THE BUTCH BAKERY COOKBOOK ::

THE BUTCH BAKERY COOKBOOK ::

DAVID ARRICK with Janice Kollar

PHOTOGRAPHY :: Jason Wyche

WILEY

JOHN WILEY & SONS, INC.

This book is printed on acid-free paper. ⊗

Copyright © 2011 by David Arrick. All rights reserved.

Photography © 2011 Jason Wyche

Food styling by Brian Preston-Campbell

Prop styling by Martha Bernabe

Graphic Design by idesign + associates, inc.

Published by John Wiley & Sons, Inc., Hoboken, New Jersey

Published simultaneously in Canada

For general information on our other products and services or for technical support, please contact our Customer Care Department within the United States at (800) 762-2974, outside the United States at (317) 572-3993 or fax (317) 572-4002.

Wiley also publishes its books in a variety of electronic formats. Some content that appears in print may not be available in electronic books. For more information about Wiley products, visit our web site at www.wiley.com.

Library of Congress Cataloging-in-Publication Data

Arrick, David.

  The Butch Bakery cookbook / David Arrick with Janice Kollar ; photography by Jason Wyche.

     p. cm.

  Includes index.

  ISBN 978-0-470-93088-5 (cloth) 978-1-118-11050-8 (ebk); 978-1-118-11051-5 (ebk); 978-1-118-11052-2 (ebk)

1. Cupcakes. 2. Cookbooks. 3. Baking. I. Kollar, Janice. II. Title.

  TX771.A76 2011

  641.8'653--dc22

                              2010041052

Printed in China

10 9 8 7 6 5 4 3 2 1

DEDICATION ::

This book is dedicated to the entrepreneur in all of us.

CONTENTS ::

ACKNOWLEDGMENTS ::

A very special thank you to our literary agent, Carla Glasser, for creating this opportunity for us, for her constant support and encouragement, and for being the best in the business.

Thanks to our wonderful editor, Justin Schwartz, for believing in this book, his insightful guidance, and standing over every phase of its development.

Thanks also to everyone involved with the "look" of the book: Jason Wyche for his delicious photos, Brian Preston-Campbell, Martha Bernabe and Levi Miller.

—David and Janice

The journey from concept to cupcakes was not always smooth, creamy, and well-blended. I need to thank the following for their support and guidance along the way:

Janice Kollar, for her incomparable talent.

My business partner, Barry Alden Clark, whose enthusiasm and spirit are unparalleled. Heidi Sadowsky, whose nurturing spirit baked the best cupcake ever—our son, Nathaniel Chase.

Mom, Dad, Robin, and Andrew, for their unconditional love and understanding.

—David

First and foremost, thanks to David for coming up with such a great idea for a cupcake company and this book, and for giving me the green light to create the recipes—what fun!

Endless thanks to the loves of my life, Zack and Bill.

I'd also like to thank Robert, Suzie, Ellen, Marie, Lainey, Austin, Ruth, Ginger, Elly, Dave, and everyone at Sunfrost Farms for their love, raves, and encouragement, and for being the best taste-testers ever. A lot of cupcakes were eaten during the creation of this book!

And finally, I must thank my grandparents, Minnie and Barney Heer, for lovingly planting and nurturing the baking seed that continues to grow on inside of me.

—Janice

INTRODUCTION :: DESSERT FOR DUDES

BUTCH MEETS BUTTERCREAM ::

Cupcakes used to be for kids, right? They were treats at children's birthday parties, not a treat for a grown-up guy. But times have changed, and cupcakes have exploded across the United States, supplying us with a sweet and inexpensive little indulgence. What became evident with some research was that even though cupcakes had grown up and become an adult treat, they were either very feminine or still looked like they were made for kids. Even with cupcake shops across the United States booming, no one had been catering to men and their particular tastes. Enter Butch Bakery. We've broken the cupcake guidelines with a roster of cupcakes that appeal to masculine taste buds, making their look streamlined and right to the point—no flowers, no swirls, no sprinkles, just a delicious frosted cupcake.

   And in this book, that's exactly what you'll find. The recipes for Butch Bakery's classic manly cupcakes are all here. And even though about half of the recipes include some kind of liquor, there are virgin suggestions included as well, so everyone can enjoy Butch Bakery cupcakes.

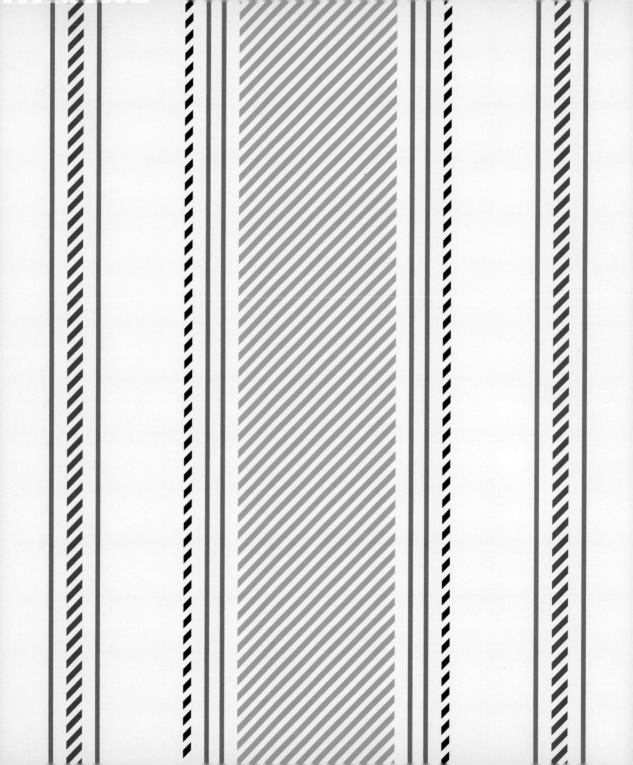

BUTCH'S CUPCAKE BOOT CAMP ::

BUTCH'S TOOLBOX ::

Any man would agree that when you're building something, you need the right tools for the job. Baking is no different, so we're including Butch's essential tool kit. You don't need all of these items, but it will make baking a lot easier, and more fun if you do.

Oven Thermometer: Now you're thinking, "What? My oven tells me what the temperature is inside the oven." And we wish we could tell you that you could trust it. But the fact is, most ovens, even high-end ones, aren't always accurate, and could vary as much as 50°F above or below what you'll need. They can also tell you that the oven is up to temperature before it really is. All of the cupcake recipes in this book need an oven set to 350°F. Be aware that an oven takes a good 15 to 20 minutes to get up to 350°F. You don't want to go to all of this trouble to find out your cupcakes are overbaked or raw in the middle, do you? We like the Taylor Classic oven thermometer; it's inexpensive and hangs under the rack out of your way. Also, ovens tend to have cool and hot spots, so it's best to rotate your pans from side to side and back to front about halfway through the baking time.

Electric Mixer: Some of Butch's recipes can be simply stirred together, but a lot of them do need a mixer. But you don't need a fancy stand mixer for these recipes. In fact, for all the recipes in this book, when we needed a mixer, we used a portable hand mixer. Frankly, we liked it that way because it was so easy to clean and store. But if you have a stand mixer on hand, certainly use it.

Wire Whisk: For the recipes that require just stirring, you could use a large spoon, but a whisk will get the job done faster. They're not expensive and a good item to have in your toolbox. One that's 8 to 10 inches long will work well. If need be, a fork will work well in a pinch.

Muffin Pans: Since our cupcakes are for men, they are also a manly size. We bake our cupcakes in jumbo-size muffin cups. For the recipes in this book, we used Wilton Ultra Bake 6-cup jumbo muffin pans. They're heavy-duty, nonstick, and not expensive. Plan on getting at least 2 pans. You can also make our cupcakes in regular-size muffin pans as well. You'll get about 18 regular-size cupcakes for every dozen of the jumbo size. Also, the baking time will be shortened by about 3 to 5 minutes.

Cupcake Liners: We love liners because they make cleanup so easy. But unlike regular-size muffin pans, jumbo-size muffin pans come in an array of sizes, which can make it difficult to find the right size liners to fit the pans. Also, grocery stores don't always carry a selection of sizes. The most readily available liner we have found is Reynolds Jumbo-Size Baking Cups, and those are the liners we used for the recipes in this book. They fit the Wilton pans perfectly and come with an aluminum foil liner attached, which means that if you like, you don't even need a muffin tin. You can just place the filled foil baking cups on a cookie sheet and bake. We still like placing the liners in the pans, though, because all of the cupcakes come out looking exactly the same size. Depending on the weight of the batter, without a muffin pan the foil may spread, creating different-shaped cupcakes.

If you can't locate these pans or liners, the amount of batter you use per cupcake may vary. Instead of using the measured amount of batter stated in the recipe (i.e., ⅓ cup), fill each cup by how full it is (i.e., ¾ full) to get the best results.

Your baking time may vary as well. So rely on your tester and how well the cupcakes spring back, as opposed to your timer.

Strainers: You'll need a medium- to large-size, medium-mesh strainer that fits over your mixing bowls for sifting your dry ingredients, and a small, fine-mesh strainer for juicing citrus.

Measuring Spoons: This does not mean the teaspoons and tablespoons in your kitchen silverware drawer. These are specifically meant for baking. One set is fine, but 2 sets are even better. Then, one set can be used for dry ingredients and the other for wet ingredients. A set consists of 1 tablespoon, 1 teaspoon. ½ teaspoon, and ¼ teaspoon. Make sure they are metal and not plastic; plastic measuring spoons are not as accurate.

Measuring Cups: At Butch's, we don't like the glass liquid measuring cups, so we never use them. We've found that a lot of times the measurement markings aren't correct. We measure all of our ingredients, including the liquids, in "dry" measuring cups, filling them right to the brim, either leveling off the dry ingredients with a knife or finger, or eyeballing the liquids. You'll use these not only for measuring ingredients, but also for scooping batter into the tins. Two sets will allow you to have one for dry ingredients and one for wet ingredients. And metal is best. A set consists of one of each of 1-cup, ½-cup, ⅓-cup, and ¼-cup measures.

Big Spoons: Used for stirring and pushing dry ingredients through the strainer.

Knives: For cutting butter and nuts. Use a small paring knife (or a melon baller) to cut holes in the top of the cupcakes, and larger knives for chopping nuts and dried fruit.

Spoonula or Rubber Spatula: You'll be scraping down the sides of the bowl for both your batter and your frosting. This makes easy work of it.

Toothpicks or Wooden Skewers: These are for testing the cupcakes for doneness. When you poke one into the center of a cupcake and it comes out clean, they're ready. You'll also use these to help speed up the soaking time by poking holes into the baked cupcakes.

Ice Cream Scoop: We use this to top our cupcakes with frosting. That way each one gets exactly the same amount of frosting, and it can neatly sit on top of the cake, ready to be topped or shined up a bit. We like the OXO Large Cookie Scoop.

Small Offset Spatula or Butter Knife: We like to use an offset spatula to shine up our cupcakes because it's easy to maneuver, but a butter knife with no serrated edges will work well, too.

Kitchen Rasp (aka Microplane): Actually, the inventor of this kitchen tool stole the idea from the tool section of the hardware store. We use it to zest (finely grate) all of our oranges, lemons, and limes. The zest is the colorful part of the fruit. Try not to grate any of the white pithy part underneath that, as it can be bitter. Always remember to zest your citrus first, before you squeeze the juice.

Citrus Reamer: You could use brute force to juice your lemons, limes, and oranges, but we prefer a wooden reamer. It's supercheap and efficient.

Wire Cooling Racks: You can't leave the cupcakes in the pans for too long. Condensation might form around them, because the air can't circulate underneath them to cool. The perfect solution is a cooling rack.

Kitchen Timer: You probably have one on your stove. If not, it's another small investment worth getting.

Food Processor: Date Night (page 143) is the only recipe in the book that requires a food processor. We wouldn't suggest that you buy one, but if you already have it, you'll love the recipe.

Crème Brûlée Torch/Small Butane Torch: Not necessary, but fun to use to roast the marshmallows on the Camp Out cupcakes (page 136) — as long as you're very careful!

Airtight Containers: Best for storage, so the cupcakes don't absorb any of the odors from the refrigerator or the freezer.

Other Useful Tools: Cutting Board: for chopping nuts, chocolate, and dried fruit. Potato Peeler: the easiest tool to use for peeling apples. Melon Baller: another way to cut holes in the top of cupcakes. Box Grater: for grating carrots and chocolate.

BUTCH'S SUPPLY CABINET ::

Now let's talk a little about ingredients.
With the exception of an extract or two,
everything you will need can be found
in your local grocery store. And again,
just like you need the right tools for the
job, you also need the right materials.
Building a house with rotten wood or
using sand for the fuel in your gas tank
is just not going to cut it.
So pay close attention here.

Flours: At the bakery we use two kinds of flour: unbleached all-purpose flour and cake flour. Make sure that the cake flour has no leavening in it—the ones with leavening are usually labeled "self-rising" cake flour.

Baking Soda and Double-Acting Baking Powder: These make the cupcakes rise, so they must be fresh. Old leaveners will not work as well. If either of these have been sitting around on your pantry shelf for more than 6 months, fling them and buy new.

Unsalted Butter: Don't get the salted variety. Not only does the amount of salt vary from brand to brand, but salt also acts as a preservative, which means that salted butter can sit in your store longer, so it might not be as fresh. With unsalted butter you can control the amount of salt that you add in a recipe, and you'll know that it's a fresher product.

Other Dairy Products: At the bakery we always use the full-fat versions for sour cream, cream cheese, and milk.

Vegetable Oil: We like to use a mild-flavored one like safflower or canola in our baking. Keep the oil refrigerated so it doesn't go rancid.

Granulated Sugar: Any brand will work here. Just don't buy superfine sugar.

Confectioners' Sugar: We use this in our buttercreams. It can get very lumpy, especially if it's older, so you need to always push it through a medium-mesh strainer with a spoon (aka sifting) after you measure it. That will ensure a creamy, lump-free frosting.

Light and Dark Brown Sugars: When purchasing brown sugar, always check to make sure that the brown sugar is soft in the bag or the box. Once it hardens, it is very difficult to soften it again. And after you use it, always squeeze the air out of the bag and reseal tightly. Our directions will instruct you to firmly pack it into the measuring cup. By that we mean that the filled cup has no air spaces, and if you inverted the cup of brown sugar onto a plate, it would hold its shape.

Unsulphured Molasses: Make sure that you don't buy blackstrap. It's too strongly flavored.

Pure Maple Syrup: Not that fake stuff, but the real thing. We like grade B. It's cheaper and more maple-y. If you can't find that, any grade will be delicious.

Light Corn Syrup: We use this to shine up our chocolate glazes. Make sure it's not dark corn syrup.

Large Eggs: Once upon a time a large egg weighed very close to 2 ounces. So a carton of one dozen eggs weighed 24 ounces. But now the rules have changed and as long as all 12 eggs add up to 24 ounces, that's considered OK. So you'll notice that some eggs in the box may be much larger and some much smaller. For baking, though, that may present a problem. If you want to have consistency in your cupcakes, try to average out the size of your eggs when you use them.

Vanilla and Other Extracts: Always, and we mean always, get the pure versions, not the artificial ones. You really can taste the difference.

Salt: We use a fine sea salt for baking. Any fine salt will do. Only use large flake or kosher varieties for sprinkling on top.

Chocolate: We use a lot of chocolate—bittersweet, semisweet, milk, and white. Everyone has his favorite brand, so choose what you like best to eat on its own. For this book, we used chips, because they're easy to measure and you don't have to go through the extra step of chopping it. But there are ounces listed in each recipe, so if you want to use bars or blocks of chocolate and weigh and chop them yourself, go right ahead.

Unsweetened Cocoa Powder: There are 2 kinds, Dutch and Natural. For our purposes, choose the cocoa that tastes the best to you. We always sift it because it can be lumpy. We use natural cocoa in all of our recipes.

Spices: We like to boost the flavor of our cupcakes any chance we get, so we use a lot of spices. After 6 months, most spices lose their potency, so it's best to toss them and buy new. But when you do, buy smaller amounts so you don't waste them.

Coffee and Espresso: We make it easy on ourselves and always use heavy doses of espresso powder for that intense coffee flavor.

Bacon: Ah, bacon. For our bacon bits we like regular sliced because it crisps up faster and stays that way. Did you know that older bacon cooks faster than fresher bacon?

Nuts: We mostly use walnuts and pecans. Be aware that the oils in the nuts can go rancid if stored at room temperature, especially during the summer months. If you have the space, it's always best to keep nuts in the freezer.

Lemons, Limes, and Oranges: Freshly squeezed is the way to go. We never use bottled. It takes a little more time, but it's beyond worth it. We use a lot of zest, too. That means finely grating the rind. Remember, it's easiest to grate before you squeeze.

Liquor and Beer: Last but not least. This is all about personal preference. In the recipes, we suggest what we like to use in the bakery, but feel free to switch them out for whatever suits your fancy.

BUTCH'S BIG BAKER'S DOZEN ::

15 STRATEGIES & PROCEDURES ::

OK. Baking can be a lot of fun, but there are some rules. If you want to be a successful cupcake-maker, you're going to have to follow the game plan. Baking is a scientific process, and must be treated as a science, period. Unlike in cooking, an error in measuring while baking can mean starting all over again from scratch. So here are a number of strategies and procedures to follow to get the best results.

1 Read the recipe from beginning to end. That way, you will not only be familiar with the recipe, but you also can make sure that you have all of the ingredients on hand before you start. There's nothing more frustrating than to find out you need 2 eggs when you only have 1 left.

2 Preheat the oven for at least 15 minutes before you bake.

3 Measure ingredients correctly!

Flours: Flour can settle if it's not used often, so it's best to stir up the flour a little before you measure it. Then, dip the dry measuring cup into the flour, and without shaking or tapping the cup, level off the top by sweeping a finger or flat knife across it.

Liquids: We measure all of the liquids in the same metal dry measuring cups. Avoid the liquid measuring cups with the spout. We have our reasons, and these recipes were created using the dry measures. Fill them right up to the top.

Measuring Spoons: These should be filled to the top. With dry ingredients, they should be evenly leveled off with a finger or on the side of the container. Don't try to eyeball small amounts. A pinch here and a pinch there will not work when you're baking.

Measuring Butter: Sometimes the markings on the wrapper are off. Make sure to measure your tablespoons by dividing the stick in half for 4 tablespoons and in half again for 2 tablespoons. Got it?

Measuring Brown Sugar: "Firmly packed" means just that. Brown sugar is always packed into dry measuring cups so that no air spaces are left. If you unmolded the brown sugar onto a plate, it would hold its shape.

Sticky Liquids: When measuring molasses and maple syrup, spray the metal measuring cup or spoon with cooking spray first, and it will slide right out.

Planning Ahead: The French have a term for measuring everything out in advance—"mise en place." If you have the time, this is the best way to go. But you can just measure as you go if you don't have the patience for that.

4 Make sure you prepare the ingredients correctly. That means that butter needs to be softened, chocolate needs to be melted and cooled, brown sugar firmly packed, confectioners' sugar sifted, etc.

5 After you measure your dry ingredients, you will almost always have to sift them. That simply means putting a medium-mesh strainer over a bowl and using a spoon to push the dry ingredients through. This will guarantee that no lumps get into your batter.

6 Softened butter: This is butter that you can make an indentation in with your finger. You don't want the butter to be so soft that it is almost a liquid.

7 Beating until light and fluffy: When working with butter, we beat it until it becomes a lighter pale yellow color and looks fluffy in the bowl. Sometimes we mix in the sugar as well and have both become light and fluffy.

8 Follow the directions to the "T." If it says beat the butter alone, do it. If it says to cool a mixture, do it. Add the ingredients according to the order in the directions.

9 Once the flour mixture is added, don't overbeat! Mix just until the dry ingredients are incorporated. Overmixing will result in a tough cupcake. We're tough, but we don't want our cupcakes to be tough.

10 Fill each prepared muffin cup with the proper amount of batter. Most of the recipes call for ¼ cup to ⅓ cup batter, either leveled off or rounded in the cup, filling each muffin cup ⅔ to no more than ¾ full. Too much batter will overflow the pans. Also, a heaping tablespoon means just that. Scoop up as much batter as the tablespoon will hold.

11 Zesting citrus fruits: Zesting means finely grating. We love our kitchen rasp (Microplane) for this job, using it for oranges, lemons, and limes. The zest is the colorful part of the fruit. Try not to grate any of the white pithy part underneath that, as it can be bitter. And always remember to zest your citrus first before you squeeze the juice.

12 Melting chocolate: We always use a small, heavy-bottomed saucepan for melting chocolate over very low heat. We stir it constantly until smooth. You can also melt chocolate in the microwave; don't do it on the highest setting, though. Place in a microwave-safe bowl, and stir every 30 seconds until smooth.

13 When are the cupcakes done? So you forgot to set the timer—no worries. We've all been there. Don't panic, just follow your nose. When you can begin to smell that delicious aroma wafting through the kitchen, it's time to check the cupcakes. They're done when the centers are springy and firm to the touch and a tester (toothpick/wooden skewer) inserted in the center of a cupcake comes out clean.

14 Cooling the proper amount of time: Let the cupcakes cool in the pans for the required time before moving them to the cooling rack. Also, make sure that the cupcakes have completely cooled before frosting them, or you'll have a mess on your hands.

15 Storing your cupcakes: If you're going to eat your cupcakes within a day or two after they're made, leave them out at room temperature and enjoy. (Cream cheese–frosted cupcakes shouldn't be at room temperature for more than 6 to 8 hours.) But if you have leftovers or need to keep them for a few days, it's best to chill them in the refrigerator, in an airtight container to keep out any undesirable odors. Freezing is another way to keep your cupcakes fresh. You can freeze the unfrosted cupcakes so they're ready to frost when you need them, or freeze them already frosted. Place them on a tray in your freezer and when frozen solid, transfer to an airtight storage container or freezer bags with the air squeezed out for up to 3 months. Unfrosted cupcakes can be defrosted at room temperature. Frosted cupcakes are best defrosted in the refrigerator. They will keep frozen for up to 1 month.

BUTCH'S CHOCOLATE DISCS ::

Our signature look for a lot of our cupcakes now, and how we got all of our attention in the first place, revolved around our chocolate discs. They're not really easy to make, but it's definitely possible to create the basic disc at home if you really want to. So we would be remiss if we didn't include the directions for making them. If you're feeling particularly ambitious, go ahead and give these a try.

THE DESIGNS FEATURED ON OUR CUSTOM-MADE CHOCOLATE DISCS ARE PRINTED ON THE CHOCOLATE WITH EDIBLE FOOD DYE. SO IF YOU WANT TO BE COMPLETELY AUTHENTIC, YOU CAN ORDER THE BUTCH BAKERY DISCS THROUGH US AT **www.butchbakery.com**

INGREDIENT AND EQUIPMENT ROSTER:

6   ounces chocolate, coarsely chopped, or 1 cup chips, any flavor that you like

Small saucepan or small microwave-safe bowl

Small metal baking pan with a very flat bottom—we like to use a ¼ sheet pan, 8 x 12 inches

Parchment paper cut to fit your pan (aluminum foil or waxed paper can be used, but parchment is best)

Scotch or masking tape

Offset spatula or nonserrated butter knife

2½-inch round cookie cutter

Small squares of parchment or large cupcake liners

Storage container

Make the Discs:

Tape a piece of parchment to the bottom side of the pan.

Melt the chocolate over very low heat in a saucepan on the stovetop, stirring constantly until smooth. Or in the microwave (not on the highest setting), heat the chocolate in a microwave-safe bowl and check every 30 seconds, stirring after each interval, until the chocolate is just smooth. Don't overheat!

Pour the chocolate onto the pan and evenly spread it quite thinly with the offset spatula to about $\frac{1}{16}$ inch thick. Place the pan in the refrigerator for 5 minutes or the freezer for 1 minute to harden. Remove and let sit for 1 minute to soften slightly.

Using the cookie cutter, gently press down and twist until it cuts through to the parchment. You want the chocolate to be soft enough not to crack but hard enough to stay firm. If the chocolate softens too quickly, chill it for 1 to 2 minutes more. Lift the disc up using the spatula so that you don't make fingerprints on the chocolate. Store between pieces of parchment in an airtight container. They will last for weeks in the refrigerator until ready to use.

The bottom of the disc (the side touching the parchment) will be smooth and will be the top of the disc on the cupcake. Transfer the discs to the finished cupcakes, using the spatula again to avoid making fingerprints.

Feel free to experiment and coat the disc with "sawdusts" (see pages 45 and 121 for examples), sugars, cocoa, etc.

PRESS ::

TWIST ::

EAT ::

1:
WORKING

WAKE-UP CALL! ::

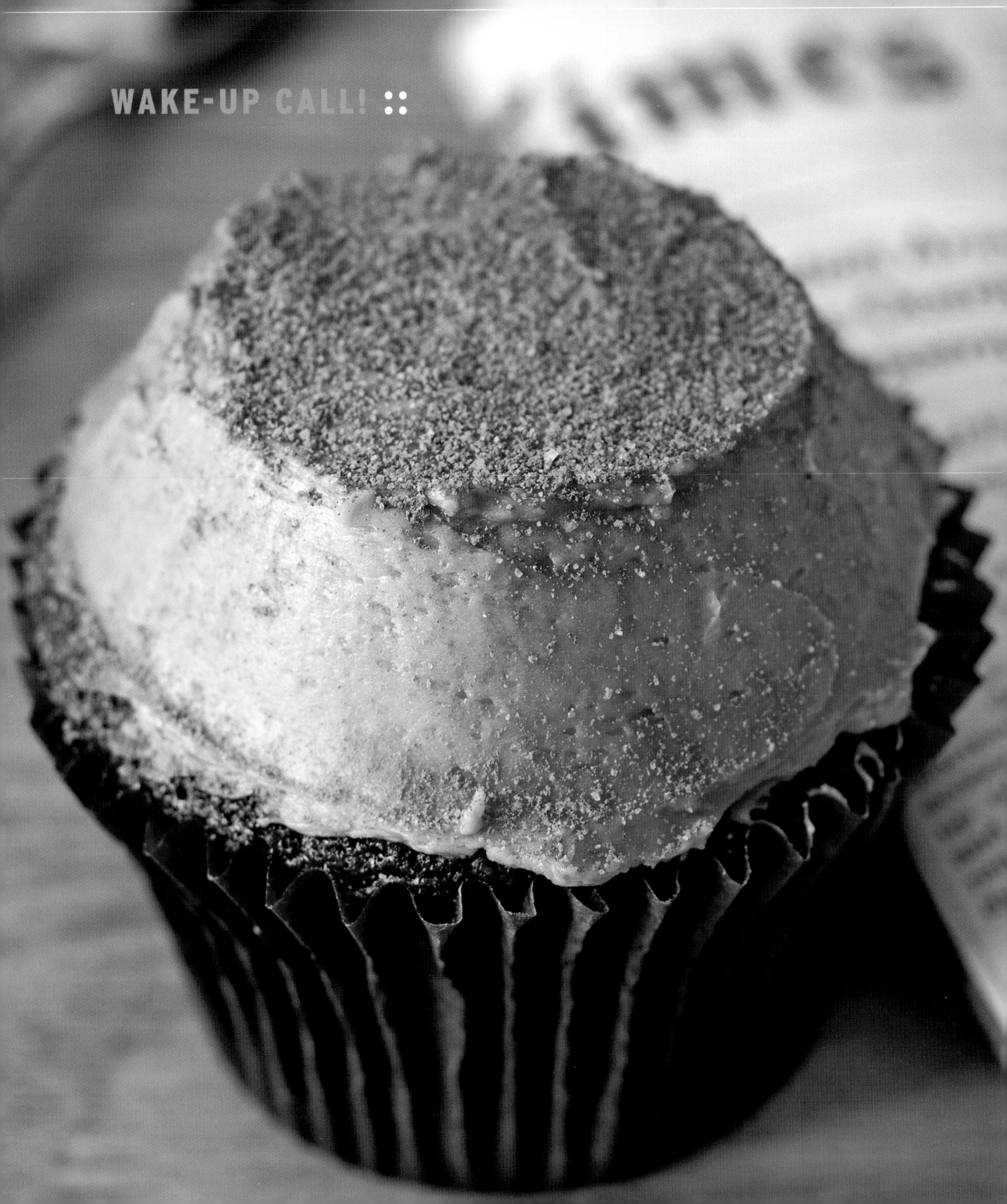

WAKE-UP CALL! ::

A Coffee-Infused Chocolate Cupcake with a Serious Coffee Buttercream
Everybody needs their cup of Joe in the morning, and at Butch's we're no different. A big hit of caffeine does just the trick first thing in the morning, or any time of day. Filled with a jolt of coffee buttercream, this coffee, and Kahlúa-spiked cupcake will get you up and running fast! **[MAKES 12 CUPCAKES]**

INGREDIENT ROSTER:

For the Coffee-Infused Chocolate Cupcakes:

- ¾ cup water
- ½ cup unsweetened cocoa powder, sifted through a strainer
- ¼ cup plus 2 tablespoons semisweet chocolate chips
- 1 tablespoon espresso powder
- 1 cup plus 2 tablespoons unbleached all-purpose flour
- 1 cup plus 2 tablespoons sugar
- ¾ teaspoon baking soda
- ½ teaspoon baking powder
- ½ teaspoon salt
- 2 large eggs, broken into a small bowl
- ¼ cup vegetable oil
- 3 tablespoons Kahlúa or other coffee-flavored liqueur
- 1½ teaspoons pure vanilla extract

For the Serious Coffee Buttercream:

- 2 tablespoons espresso powder
- 1½ tablespoons Kahlúa or other coffee-flavored liqueur
- 1½ tablespoons unsweetened cocoa powder
- 1½ tablespoons pure vanilla extract
- Pinch salt
- 12 ounces (3 sticks) unsalted butter, softened
- 3¾ cups confectioners' sugar, sifted through a strainer
- 3 tablespoons egg substitute, like Egg Beaters

Toppings: (optional)

Chocolate Sawdust (recipe follows)
Coffee Sawdust (recipe follows)

PLAN OF ATTACK:

Make the Cupcakes: Place a baking rack in the center of the oven and preheat the oven to 350°F. Line two 6-cup jumbo-size muffin pans with liners and set aside.

In a small saucepan, bring the water to a boil and remove from the heat. Stir in the cocoa powder, chocolate chips, and espresso powder, and stir until smooth. Set aside to cool, about 20 minutes.

In a medium-size mixing bowl, add the flour, sugar, baking soda, baking powder, and salt. Whisk to combine. Add the eggs, oil, Kahlúa, vanilla, and the chocolate/espresso mixture to the bowl, whisking just until all of the ingredients are completely incorporated.

Fill each prepared muffin cup with $\frac{1}{4}$ cup batter, about $\frac{2}{3}$ full. Bake, rotating the pans halfway through, until the tops are just firm to the touch and a tester inserted in the center of a cupcake comes out clean, about 23 minutes. Leave the cupcakes in the pan on a rack to cool for 5 to 10 minutes. Transfer the cupcakes to the wire rack to cool completely before frosting, about 1 hour.

Make the Buttercream: In a small bowl, combine the espresso powder, Kahlúa, cocoa powder, vanilla, and salt. Stir the mixture until the espresso and cocoa powders are dissolved and set aside.

In a large-size mixing bowl, with an electric mixer on medium-high speed, beat the butter until light and fluffy, 2 to 3 minutes. Scrape down the sides of the bowl, and add the confectioners' sugar and egg substitute, beating on medium-low to combine. Add the coffee/cocoa mixture, and continue beating on medium-high for 2 to 3 minutes until very smooth and creamy, scraping down the sides of the bowl as needed.

Cupcake Construction: Get out that ice cream scoop (2 to $2\frac{1}{4}$ inches in diameter) and top each cupcake with a generous rounded scoop of frosting. Sprinkle the tops with $\frac{1}{4}$ to $\frac{1}{2}$ teaspoon of the sawdust of your choice, if desired. Cupcakes can be refrigerated for up to 3 days in an airtight container, or frozen for 1 month.

If You Like: Before sprinkling a topping, you can shine the cupcakes up a bit by taking a butter knife (no serrated edges, please) and pushing the frosting down to about an inch high, flattening the top, and then taking the knife and making a flat 45-degree angled edge all the way around the side of the scoop of frosting.

Virgin Wake-Up Call: Substitute regular coffee or espresso for the coffee liqueur.

Chocolate Sawdust: In a small bowl, mix together 2 tablespoons sugar plus 1 teaspoon cocoa powder.

Coffee Sawdust: In a small bowl, mix together 2 tablespoons sugar plus ½ teaspoon espresso powder.

MIX AND MATCH: Wake-Up Call!'s Cake with Coffee Break's Double-Shot Espresso Buttercream (page 56)

   Wake-Up Call! Buttercream with No-Hitter's Kick-Ass Yellow Cake (page 89)

....

[BUTCH'S BAKING LESSON] Read the whole recipe from start to finish before you begin to bake. We know it's tempting to just dive in there, but you need to know what you're doing first. Plus, this gives you a chance to make sure that you have all of the ingredients on hand. It's a real bummer to find out after you've started making a recipe that you don't have any eggs around. There's a reason that there's a recipe, so follow it!

DRILLER ::

A Maple Cupcake frosted with Milk Chocolate Ganache and Butch's Bacon Bits

Maple syrup—sweet, syrupy, and so good in these cupcakes. They're topped with a mound of milk chocolate and sprinkled with our bacon bits. What's not to love? We like to chop up the bacon really fine—but if you prefer big chunks on top, we say go for it! You're going to need a mixer, and the butter has to be soft—don't even think of starting with cold butter. But you'll be drillin' through this recipe in no time. Oh, and don't be scared off by the word "ganache." It's just another name for delicious, creamy frosting. **[MAKES 12 CUPCAKES]**

INGREDIENT ROSTER:

For the Maple Cupcakes:

- 2 cups unbleached all-purpose flour
- 1½ teaspoons baking powder
- ¼ teaspoon salt
- 10 tablespoons (1¼ sticks) unsalted butter, softened
- 1 cup firmly packed light brown sugar
- 3 large eggs, broken into a small bowl
- 2 teaspoons pure vanilla extract
- ⅓ cup whole milk
- ⅓ cup pure maple syrup

For the Milk Chocolate Ganache:

- 4 tablespoons (½ stick) unsalted butter
- 1 cup heavy cream
- 1½ cups milk chocolate chips
- ½ cup semisweet chocolate chips
- ½ teaspoon pure vanilla extract
- Pinch salt

Topping:

- ¾ cup Butch's Bacon Bits (recipe follows) or crumbled crisp bacon

PLAN OF ATTACK:

Make the Cupcakes: Place a baking rack in the center of the oven and preheat the oven to 350°F. Line two 6-cup jumbo-size muffin pans with liners and set aside.

Place a strainer over a medium mixing bowl and sift together the flour, baking powder, and salt. Set aside.

In a medium-size mixing bowl, with an electric mixer on medium-high speed, beat the butter and brown sugar until well combined. Add the eggs and vanilla and beat until creamy. Scrape down the sides of the bowl and add half of the flour mixture and the milk, beating to combine. Add the rest of the flour mixture and the maple syrup, and continue to mix just until the dry ingredients are incorporated, scraping down the sides of the bowl as needed.

Fill each prepared muffin cup with a rounded ⅓ cup batter, about ¾ full. Bake, rotating the pans halfway through, until the tops are just firm to the touch and a tester inserted in the center of a cupcake comes out clean, about 24 minutes. Leave the cupcakes in the pan on a rack to cool for 5 to 10 minutes. Transfer the cupcakes to the wire rack to cool completely before frosting, about 1 hour.

Make the Ganache: In heavy 2-quart saucepan over low heat, melt the butter. Stir in the cream and heat until very hot but not boiling. Remove from the stove and stir in both kinds of chocolate chips until smooth and glossy. Stir in the vanilla and the salt. Transfer to a medium-size mixing bowl, and cool to room temperature. Chilling the mixture in the refrigerator will take about 1 hour. Beat the ganache on medium-high speed until thick and creamy, about 2 to 3 minutes.

Cupcake Construction: Get out that ice cream scoop (2 to 2¼ inches) and top each cupcake with a generous rounded scoop of frosting. Sprinkle 1 rounded teaspoon of the bacon bits on top of each cupcake. Cupcakes can be refrigerated for up to 3 days in an airtight container, or frozen for 1 month.

If You Like: You can shine them up a bit before you sprinkle on the bacon bits by taking a butter knife (no serrated edges, please) and pushing the frosting down to about an inch high, flattening the top, and then taking the knife and making a flat 45-degree angled edge all the way around the side of the scoop of frosting.

Optional Frosting Suggestion: The milk chocolate ganache can be used when warm, too. Just spoon it over the cupcakes as a glaze and let cool on the cupcakes. You won't get as much frosting on top, but you'll be able to eat them much sooner—with no mixer to clean!

MIX AND MATCH: Driller's Cakes with 4&10's Peanutty Buttercream (page 105)
Driller's Ganache with Home Run's Peanut Butter Cake (page 71)

Butch's Bacon Bits:

⅓ cup firmly packed light brown sugar

⅛ teaspoon ground black pepper

10 to 12 slices of regular-cut bacon
(½ pound)

Preheat the oven to 400°F and adjust the rack in the upper half of the oven. Line a rimmed baking sheet with aluminum foil and place a similar-sized wire cooling rack inside the pan.

In a medium-size mixing bowl, combine the brown sugar and pepper. Add the bacon strips and toss in the mixture. Lay the strips in one layer on the rack and top with any leftover sugar. Bake for 25 to 30 minutes until browned. Cool slightly before finely chopping. This will keep for 1 week stored in an airtight container in the refrigerator.

[MAKES ABOUT ¾ CUP]

....

[BUTCH'S BAKING LESSON] Baking is a science! So make sure that you always measure your ingredients correctly. Mess that up and you're not going to get the results you're expecting. Remember, at Butch's, we use dry metal measuring cups for liquid and dry ingredients. Dry ingredients are overfilled and then leveled off, and liquids are filled right to the brim. Don't forget to fill your measuring spoons right to the tops, too.

JACK HAMMER ::

JACK HAMMER ::

A Vanilla-Buttermilk Cupcake with Chocolate-Hazelnut Filling and Buttercream
At Butch's we weren't that familiar with this combination. Chocolate and hazelnuts? But then Barry brought in a jar of Nutella one day, and we were all hooked, eating it by the spoonful until the jar was empty! And the next thing ya know, we had the Jack Hammer. We even throw a dollop of Nutella into the center of these cupcakes as they bake. We just can't get enough! You're gonna need 2 jars for this one. **[MAKES 12 CUPCAKES]**

INGREDIENT ROSTER:

For the Vanilla-Buttermilk Cupcakes:

- 1½ cups cake flour
- ½ cup unbleached all-purpose flour
- 1 teaspoon baking powder
- ¾ teaspoon baking soda
- ½ teaspoon salt
- 8 tablespoons (1 stick) unsalted butter, softened
- 1 cup sugar
- 2 large eggs, broken into a small bowl
- 2 teaspoons pure vanilla extract
- 1 cup well-shaken buttermilk
- ¼ cup Nutella

For the Chocolate-Hazelnut Buttercream:

- 8 tablespoons (1 stick) unsalted butter, softened
- 1 cup Nutella
- 2 cups confectioners' sugar, sifted through a strainer
- ¼ cup heavy cream

Toppings: (optional)

- ¼ cup chopped hazelnuts
- ¼ cup grated milk chocolate

PLAN OF ATTACK:

Make the Cupcakes: Place a baking rack in the center of the oven and preheat the oven to 350°F. Line two 6-cup jumbo-size muffin pans with liners and set aside.

Place a strainer over a medium-size mixing bowl and sift together the cake flour, baking powder, baking soda, and salt. Set aside.

In another medium-size mixing bowl, with an electric mixer on medium-high speed, beat the butter and sugar together until light and fluffy, 2 to 3 minutes. Scrape down the sides of the bowl, and add the eggs and vanilla, beating until combined. Add the flour mixture and buttermilk and beat on low speed, just until all the dry ingredients are incorporated, scraping down the sides of the bowl as needed.

Reserve ¾ cup of the batter. Fill each prepared muffin cup with ⅓ cup batter, about ⅔ full. Top each with 1 rounded teaspoon of Nutella and then cover with 1 tablespoon of the reserved batter. Bake, rotating the pans halfway through, until the tops are just firm to the touch and a tester inserted in the center of a cupcake comes out clean, about 23 minutes. Leave the cupcakes in the pan on a rack to cool for 5 to 10 minutes. Transfer the cupcakes to the wire rack to cool completely before frosting, about 1 hour.

Make the Buttercream: In a large-size mixing bowl, with an electric mixer on medium-high speed, beat the butter and the Nutella until combined. Scrape down the sides of the bowl, and add the confectioners' sugar and cream. Beat on medium-high speed for 2 to 3 minutes until very smooth and creamy, scraping down the sides of the bowl as needed.

Cupcake Construction: Get out that ice cream scoop (2 to 2¼ inches in diameter) and top each cupcake with a generous rounded scoop of frosting. Sprinkle with 1 teaspoon each of the chopped hazelnuts and grated milk chocolate, if desired. Cupcakes can be refrigerated for up to 3 days in an airtight container, or frozen for 1 month.

If You Like: Before you sprinkle on the toppings, you can shine the cupcakes up a bit by taking a butter knife (no serrated edges, please) and pushing the frosting down to about an inch high, flattening the top, and then taking the knife and making a flat 45-degree angled edge all the way around the side of the scoop of frosting.

MIX AND MATCH: Jack Hammer's Cake with Kick-Off's Vanilla-Spiked Cream Cheese Frosting (page 98)

Jack Hammer's Buttercream with B-52's Kahlúa-Soaked Yellow Cake (page 64)

[NOTES]

_____

_____

_____

_____

_____

_____

_____

_____

....

[BUTCH'S BAKING LESSON] Measuring flour should be easy, right? And it is, but there's one trick to follow. Always stir your flour in the canister or bag first, and then spoon it into the measuring cup without shaking or tapping it down into the cup. Then use a flat knife or your finger to level off the top of the cup. Flour can compress while it's sitting around, which means you'll have too much flour in your recipe. So remember to stir it first!

"It's a real bummer to find out after you've started baking that you don't have any eggs around. There's a reason that there's a recipe, so follow it!"

COFFEE BREAK ::

An Espresso- and Kahlúa-Infused Cupcake with a Double Shot of Espresso Buttercream It's the middle of the afternoon, and you're draggin'. The perfect pick-me-up? A big boost of caffeine. These cupcakes will deliver that kick every time. They're loaded with Kahlúa and espresso—a full cup of espresso in each one! **[MAKES 12 CUPCAKES]**

INGREDIENT ROSTER:

For the Espresso- and Kahlúa-Infused Cupcakes:

- 12 tablespoons (1½ sticks) unsalted butter
- ¾ cup water
- 3 tablespoons espresso powder
- 2 large eggs, broken into a small bowl
- ¼ cup Kahlúa or other coffee-flavored liqueur
- 2 tablespoons whole milk
- 1½ teaspoons pure vanilla extract
- ¾ teaspoon baking soda
- 1½ cups unbleached all-purpose flour
- 1½ cups sugar
- ¼ teaspoon salt

For the Double-Shot Espresso Buttercream:

- 2 tablespoons espresso powder
- 1 tablespoon Kahlúa or other coffee-flavored liqueur
- 1 tablespoon pure vanilla extract
- Pinch salt
- 8 ounces (2 sticks) unsalted butter, softened
- 2½ cups confectioners' sugar, sifted through a strainer
- 2 tablespoons egg substitute, like Egg Beaters

Toppings: (optional)

- Coffee Sawdust (recipe follows)
- Chocolate-Covered Coffee Bean Sawdust (recipe follows)

PLAN OF ATTACK:

Make the Cupcakes: Place a baking rack in the center of the oven and preheat the oven to 350°F. Line two 6-cup jumbo-size muffin pans with liners and set aside.

In a small saucepan over medium heat, melt the butter. Add the water and espresso powder to the pot, stirring to dissolve the espresso. Bring the mixture to a boil, and remove from the heat to cool slightly, about 15 minutes.

In a medium-size mixing bowl, add the eggs, Kahlúa, milk, vanilla, and baking soda. Whisk to combine. Add the flour, sugar, salt, and butter mixture to the bowl and whisk again, just until all of the ingredients are completely incorporated. Don't worry, the batter will be thin.

Fill each prepared muffin cup with ⅓ cup batter, about ⅔ full. Bake, rotating the pans halfway through, until the tops are just firm to the touch and a tester inserted in the center of a cupcake comes out clean, about 24 minutes. Leave the cupcakes in the pan on a rack to cool for 5 to 10 minutes. Transfer the cupcakes to the wire rack to cool completely before frosting, about 1 hour.

Make the Buttercream: In a small bowl, add the espresso powder, Kahlúa, vanilla, and salt. Stir until the espresso and salt are dissolved and set aside.

In a large-size mixing bowl, with an electric mixer on medium-high speed, beat the butter until light and fluffy, 2 to 3 minutes. Scrape down the sides of the bowl, and add the confectioners' sugar and egg substitute, beating on medium-low to combine. Add the Kahlúa mixture, and continue beating on medium-high speed for 2 to 3 minutes until very smooth and creamy, scraping down the sides of the bowl as needed.

Cupcake Construction: Now get out that ice cream scoop (2 to 2¼ inches in diameter) and top each cupcake with a generous rounded scoop of frosting. Sprinkle with Coffee Sawdust or Chocolate-Covered Coffee Bean Sawdust, if desired. Cupcakes can be refrigerated for up to 3 days in an airtight container, or frozen for 1 month.

If You Like: Before sprinkling the tops, you can shine them up a bit by taking a butter knife (no serrated edges, please) and pushing the frosting down to about an inch high, flattening the top, and then taking the knife and making a flat 45-degree angled edge all the way around the side of the scoop of frosting.

Virgin Coffee Break: For the Kahlúa, substitute regular coffee or espresso.

Coffee Sawdust: In a small bowl, stir together 2 tablespoons sugar plus ½ teaspoon espresso powder, combining well.

Chocolate-Covered Coffee Bean Sawdust: Whiz 3 tablespoons chocolate-covered coffee beans in a coffee grinder until finely ground.

MIX AND MATCH: Coffee Break's Cake with B-52's Bailey's Buttercream (page 64)
Coffee Break's Buttercream with Wake-Up Call's Coffee-Infused Chocolate Cake (page 43)

[BUTCH'S BAKING LESSON] What is softened butter? This can be confusing, because depending on the temperature of your kitchen, the butter may be softer one day than another. As a rule of thumb, you want to be able to leave an impression with your finger when the stick of butter is lightly pressed. It will still be a little cool, around 70°F. It shouldn't be so soft that it's almost melting.

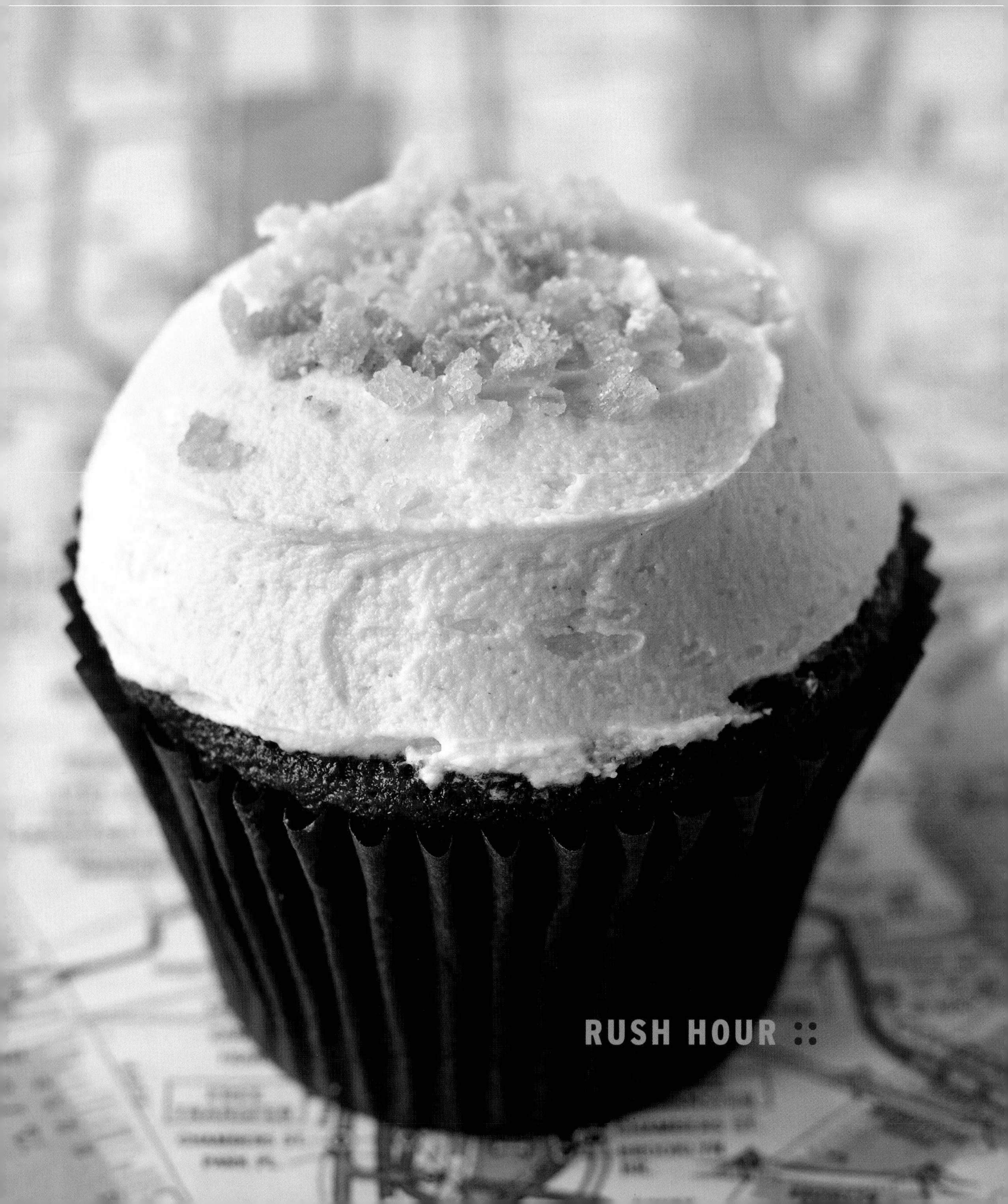

RUSH HOUR ::

RUSH HOUR ::

A Stout-Spiked Gingerbread Cupcake topped with Ginger Buttercream
These cupcakes have zing! There's a serious amount of ginger in these gingerbread cupcakes—enough to get your motor running. At first we thought, we've gone too far this time. There's way too much in there. But everyone who tried them didn't think so at all. As a matter of fact, they loved them! We've added some beer to smooth them out just a little, but not too much. And then, topping them with ginger buttercream seemed to be the best way to complete the picture. We're sure you'll agree.

[MAKES 12 CUPCAKES]

INGREDIENT ROSTER:

For the Stout-Spiked Gingerbread
Cupcakes:

- 2 cups cake flour
- 1½ teaspoons baking soda
- 2 tablespoons ground ginger
- 2 teaspoons ground cinnamon
- ½ teaspoon ground cloves
- ¾ teaspoon salt
- 1 cup firmly packed dark brown sugar
- ½ cup mild vegetable oil
- ½ cup unsulphured molasses
- 2 large eggs, broken into a small bowl
- 1 teaspoon pure vanilla extract
- ½ cup stout beer, such as Guinness, poured and settled before you measure

For the Ginger Buttercream:

- 8 ounces (2 sticks) unsalted butter, softened
- 3 cups confectioners' sugar, sifted through a strainer
- 1½ tablespoons heavy cream
- ¾ teaspoon ground ginger
- ½ teaspoon pure vanilla extract
- Pinch salt

Toppings: (optional)

- Ginger Sawdust (recipe follows)
- ¼ cup chopped crystallized ginger

PLAN OF ATTACK:

Make the Cupcakes: Place a baking rack in the center of the oven and preheat the oven to 350°F. Line two 6-cup jumbo-size muffin pans with liners and set aside.

Place a strainer over a medium-size mixing bowl and sift together the cake flour, baking soda, ginger, cinnamon, cloves, and salt. Set aside.

In another medium-size mixing bowl, whisk together the brown sugar, oil, molasses, eggs, and vanilla until creamy. Whisk in the flour mixture, combining well. In a small saucepan, heat the beer almost to boiling, and slowly add to the batter, stirring well to incorporate. The batter will be thin.

Fill each prepared muffin cup with ⅓ cup batter, about ⅔ full. Bake, rotating the pans halfway through, until the tops are just firm to the touch and a tester inserted in the center of a cupcake comes out clean, about 23 minutes. Leave the cupcakes in the pan on a rack to cool for 5 to 10 minutes. Transfer the cupcakes to the wire rack to cool completely before frosting, about 1 hour.

Make the Buttercream: In a large-size mixing bowl, using an electric mixer on medium-high speed, beat the butter until light and fluffy. Scrape down the sides of the bowl, reduce the speed to medium, and add half of the confectioners' sugar, the heavy cream, ginger, vanilla, and salt, beating to incorporate. Add the rest of the confectioners' sugar, beating on medium-high for 2 to 3 minutes until very smooth and creamy, scraping down the sides of the bowl as needed.

Cupcake Construction: Get out that ice cream scoop (2 to 2¼ inches in diameter) and top each cupcake with frosting. Sprinkle the tops with ¼ teaspoon Ginger Sawdust or 1 teaspoon chopped crystallized ginger, if desired. Cupcakes can be refrigerated for up to 3 days in an airtight container, or frozen for 1 month.

If You Like: Before sprinkling the tops, you can shine them up a bit by taking a butter knife (no serrated edges, please) and pushing the frosting down to about an inch high, flattening the top, and then taking the knife and making a flat 45-degree angled edge all the way around the side of the scoop of frosting.

Virgin Rush Hour: In the gingerbread, substitute ginger ale for the stout.

Ginger Sawdust: In a small bowl, mix together 2 tablespoons sugar with ½ teaspoon ground ginger.

MIX AND MATCH: Rush Hour's Cake with Beer Run's Vanilla Stout Buttercream (page 81)
Rush Hour's Buttercream with Big Papi's Spiced-Up Cake (page 127)

[NOTES]

_____

_____

_____

_____

_____

_____

_____

_____

_____

[BUTCH'S BAKING LESSON] Here's a trick to get all of the molasses out of the measuring cup. Spray the cup with cooking spray first, and it will slide right out!

B-52 ::

A Kahlúa-Soaked Yellow Cupcake with Bailey's Buttercream

Irish coffee is a favorite after-dinner drink around here, especially on cold winter nights. So making an Irish coffee cupcake was totally agreed upon by everyone in the bakery. You can make an Irish coffee with heavy cream and Irish whiskey, but we think it's essential to use Bailey's Irish Cream in this drink. We soak the cupcake with coffee-flavored Kahlúa, and we insist on having Bailey's in our frosting. **[MAKES 12 CUPCAKES]**

INGREDIENT ROSTER:

For the Yellow Cupcakes:

- 2 cups cake flour
- 1 teaspoon baking powder
- ¾ teaspoon baking soda
- ½ teaspoon salt
- 8 tablespoons (1 stick) unsalted butter, softened
- 1 cup sugar
- 2 large eggs, broken into a small bowl
- 2 teaspoons pure vanilla extract
- 1 cup well-shaken buttermilk

For the Bailey's Buttercream:

- 8 tablespoons (1 stick) unsalted butter, softened
- 3½ cups confectioners' sugar, sifted through a strainer
- ¼ cup plus 2 tablespoons Bailey's Irish Cream
- Pinch salt

For the Soaking Liquid:

- ¾ to 1 cup Kahlúa or another coffee-flavored liqueur

PLAN OF ATTACK:

Make the Cupcakes: Place a baking rack in the center of the oven and preheat the oven to 350°F. Line two 6-cup jumbo-size muffin pans with liners and set aside.

Place a strainer over a medium-size mixing bowl and sift together the cake flour, baking powder, baking soda, and salt. Set aside.

In another medium-size mixing bowl, with an electric mixer on medium-high speed, beat the butter and sugar together until light and fluffy. Scrape down the sides of the bowl and add the eggs and vanilla, beating until well combined. Add the flour mixture and the buttermilk, beating on low speed, mixing just until all of the dry ingredients are completely incorporated, scraping down the sides of the bowl as needed.

Fill each prepared muffin cup with a rounded $1/3$ cup batter, about $3/4$ full. Bake, rotating the pans halfway through, until the tops are just firm to the touch and a tester inserted in the center of a cupcake comes out clean, about 22 minutes. Leave the cupcakes in the pan on a rack to cool for 5 to 10 minutes. Transfer the cupcakes to the wire rack to cool completely before frosting, about 1 hour.

Make the Buttercream: In a large-size mixing bowl, with an electric mixer on medium-high speed, beat the butter until light and fluffy. Scrape down the sides of the bowl, reduce the speed to medium, and add half of the confectioners' sugar, Bailey's, and salt, beating to incorporate. Add the rest of the confectioners' sugar, beating on medium-high speed for 2 to 3 minutes until very smooth and creamy, scraping down the sides of the bowl as needed.

Cupcake Construction: Slowly spoon 1 to $1^1/2$ tablespoons of Kahlúa over the top of each cupcake. Let them sit for 10 minutes to allow the Kahlúa to be absorbed. Then get out that ice cream scoop (2 to $2^1/4$ inches in diameter) and top each cupcake with a generous rounded scoop of frosting. Cupcakes can be refrigerated for up to 3 days in an airtight container, or frozen for 1 month.

If You Like: You can shine them up a bit by taking a butter knife (no serrated edges, please) and pushing the frosting down to about an inch high, flattening the top, and then taking the knife and making a flat 45-degree angled edge all the way around the side of the scoop of frosting.

MIX AND MATCH: B-52's Cake with Wake-Up Call's Serious Coffee Buttercream (page 43)
B-52's Buttercream with Coffee Break's Espresso and Kahlúa-Infused Cake (page 56)

[NOTES]

_____

_____

_____

_____

_____

_____

_____

_____

_____

_____

[BUTCH'S BAKING LESSON] So you don't have any cake flour. Not a problem. For 1 cup cake flour, measure 2 tablespoons cornstarch into a 1-cup measure and fill to the top with unbleached all-purpose flour. Or if you don't have cornstarch on hand, just use $7/8$ cup (1 cup minus 2 tablespoons) flour for every 1 cup cake flour.

B-52 ::

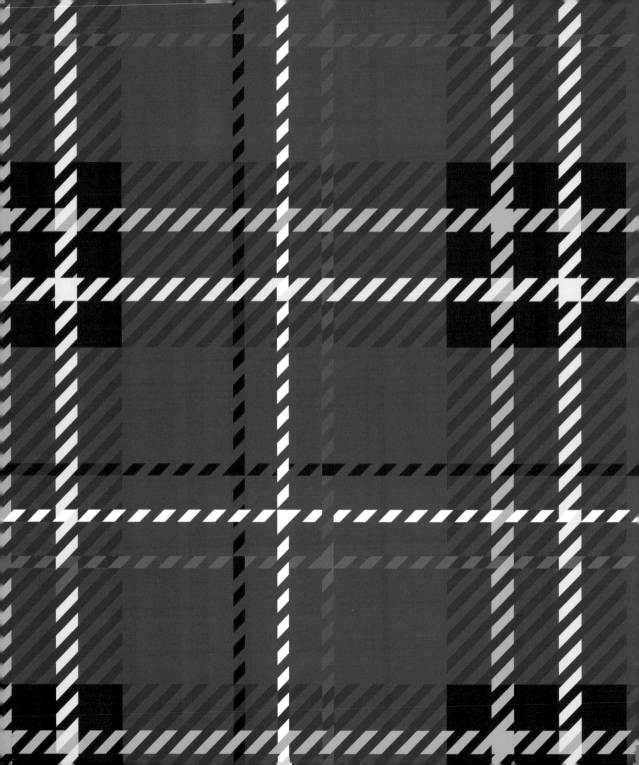

2:
PLAY BALL!

HOME RUN

HOME RUN ::

A Peanut Butter Cupcake with Banana Buttercream topped with Butch's Bacon Bits Guys like peanut butter, but jelly? Bananas, though, are another story completely. Peanut butter and bananas are a match made in heaven. This rich peanut butter cupcake is topped with a super creamy banana buttercream—a favorite at Butch's Bakery. What makes them a Home Run? Why, Butch's Crispy Bacon Bits on top, of course! **[MAKES 12 CUPCAKES]**

INGREDIENT ROSTER:

For the Peanut Butter Cupcakes:

- 1½ cups unbleached all-purpose flour
- 1½ teaspoons baking powder
- ½ teaspoon salt
- 9 tablespoons unsalted butter, softened
- 1 cup sugar
- ¾ cup creamy peanut butter (not freshly ground)
- 3 large eggs, broken into a small bowl
- ½ cup whole milk
- 2 teaspoons pure vanilla extract

For the Banana Buttercream:

- 8 tablespoons (1 stick) unsalted butter, softened
- ¼ cup mashed ripe banana, about 1 small banana
- 1 tablespoon plus 1 teaspoon banana liqueur
- 3½ cups confectioners' sugar, sifted through a strainer

Fizzy Banana Filling: (optional)

- 2 to 3 tablespoons lemon-lime soda
- 2 large ripe bananas, cut into ¼-inch rounds

Topping:

- ¾ cup Butch's Bacon Bits (recipe follows), or crumbled crisp bacon

PLAN OF ATTACK:

Make the Cupcakes: Place a baking rack in the center of the oven and preheat the oven to 350°F. Line two 6-cup jumbo-size muffin pans with liners and set aside.

Place a strainer over a medium-size mixing bowl and sift together the flour, baking powder, and salt. Set aside.

In a medium-size mixing bowl, with an electric mixer on medium-high speed, beat the butter, sugar, and peanut butter until creamy. Scrape down the sides of the bowl and add the eggs, milk, and vanilla, beating until well combined. Add the flour mixture, beating on low speed, mixing just until all of the dry ingredients are completely incorporated, scraping down the sides of the bowl as needed. The batter will be thick.

Fill each prepared muffin cup with a rounded $\frac{1}{3}$ cup batter, about $\frac{3}{4}$ full, smoothing the tops. Bake, rotating the pans halfway through, until the tops are just firm to the touch and a tester inserted in the center of a cupcake comes out clean, about 25 minutes. Leave the cupcakes in the pan on a rack to cool for 5 to 10 minutes. Transfer the cupcakes to the wire rack to cool completely before frosting, about 1 hour.

Make the Buttercream: In a medium-size mixing bowl, with an electric mixer on medium-high speed, beat the butter until light and fluffy, about 1 minute. Scrape down the sides of the bowl and add the mashed banana, banana liqueur, and half of the confectioners' sugar, and beat to combine. Add the rest of the confectioners' sugar, continuing to beat on medium-high speed until very smooth and creamy for 2 to 3 minutes more, scraping down the sides of the bowl as needed.

Cupcake Construction: If using the fizzy banana filling, with a small knife, carve a 2 x 2-inch hole in the top of each cupcake. Sprinkle the soda over the banana slices, toss to coat, and fill each hole with 5 to 6 slices of banana. Then get out that ice cream scoop (2 to $2\frac{1}{4}$ inches in diameter) and top each cupcake with frosting. Sprinkle each cupcake with 2 teaspoons of the bacon bits. Cupcakes can be refrigerated for up to 3 days in an airtight container, or frozen for 1 month.

If You Like: You can shine them up a bit before you sprinkle on the bacon bits by taking a butter knife (no serrated edges, please) and pushing the frosting down to about an inch high, flattening the top, and then taking the knife and making a flat 45-degree angled edge all the way around the side of the scoop of frosting.

MIX AND MATCH: Home Run's Cake with No-Hitter's Best Chocolate Buttercream (page 89)

Home Run's Buttercream with 4&10's Chocolate Chip Banana Cake (page 105)

Butch's Bacon Bits:

- ⅓ **cup firmly packed light brown sugar**
- ⅛ **teaspoon ground black pepper**
- 10 **to 12 slices of regular-cut bacon**
   (½ pound)

Preheat the oven to 400°F and adjust the rack in the upper half of the oven. Line a rimmed baking sheet with aluminum foil and place a similar-sized wire cooling rack inside the pan.

In a medium-size mixing bowl, combine the brown sugar and pepper. Add the bacon strips and toss in the mixture. Lay the strips in one layer on the rack and top with any leftover sugar. Bake for 25 to 30 minutes until browned. Cool slightly before finely chopping. This will keep for 1 week stored in an airtight container in the refrigerator.

[MAKES ABOUT ¾ CUP]

....

[BUTCH'S BAKING LESSON] You'll notice that we said to not use freshly ground peanut butter. Although it's great on bread, it's not so good in your cupcakes because the fresh version doesn't react well to the baking process.

REALLY HOT DOG ::

A Chile-Spiked Devil's Food Cupcake topped with Dark and White Chocolate–Chile Buttercream This is about as devilish as a chocolate cake can become. It's loaded with chocolate, sour cream, and butter, and for that devilish kick—a hit of cayenne in both the cake and the buttercream. Plus that hint of white chocolate in the buttercream makes it all go down nice and easy. We're giving you a range of heat so you can choose just how hot you want to go. In the bakery we use ½ to ¾ teaspoon in both. This cupcake version of a double-chocolate devil dog will bark that old dog back into his yard.

[MAKES 12 CUPCAKES]

INGREDIENT ROSTER:

For the Chile-Spiked Devil's Food Cupcakes:

- ¾ cup water
- ½ cup unsweetened cocoa powder, sifted through a strainer
- ⅔ cup unbleached all-purpose flour
- ½ cup cake flour
- 1 teaspoon baking powder
- ½ teaspoon baking soda
- ½ to 1 teaspoon cayenne powder, you decide
- ¼ teaspoon salt
- 10 tablespoons (1¼ sticks) butter, softened
- 1 cup firmly packed light brown sugar
- 2 large eggs, broken into a small bowl
- ¼ cup full-fat sour cream
- 1 teaspoon pure vanilla extract

For the Dark and White Chocolate–Chile Buttercream:

- 1 cup bittersweet chocolate chips (6 ounces)
- ⅔ cup white chocolate (4 ounces)
- 10 ounces (2½ sticks) unsalted butter, softened
- 2⅔ cups confectioners' sugar, sifted through a strainer
- ¼ cup heavy cream
- 1 teaspoon pure vanilla extract
- ½ to 1 teaspoon cayenne powder, you decide
- Pinch salt

PLAN OF ATTACK:

Make the Cupcakes: Place a baking rack in the center of the oven and preheat the oven to 350°F. Line two 6-cup jumbo-size muffin pans with liners and set aside.

In a small saucepan, boil the water, remove the pan from the heat, and stir in the cocoa powder until smooth. Set aside to cool slightly.

Place a strainer over a medium-size mixing bowl and sift together the all-purpose flour, cake flour, baking powder, baking soda, cayenne powder, and salt. Set aside.

In another medium-size mixing bowl, using an electric mixer on medium-high speed, beat the butter and brown sugar together until well combined, 2 to 3 minutes. Scrape down the sides of the bowl and add the eggs, sour cream, and vanilla, beating until combined. Don't worry if the mixture looks curdled. Add the flour and cocoa mixtures, beating on low speed just until all the dry ingredients are incorporated, scraping down the sides of the bowl as needed.

Fill each prepared muffin cup with ⅓ cup batter, about ⅔ full. Bake, rotating the pans halfway through, until the tops are just firm to the touch and a tester inserted in the center of a cupcake comes out clean, about 25 minutes. Leave the cupcakes in the pan on a rack to cool for 5 to 10 minutes. Transfer the cupcakes to the wire rack to cool completely before frosting, about 1 hour.

Make the Buttercream: In a small saucepan over very low heat, melt the bittersweet and white chocolates, stirring constantly until smooth. Alternatively, place both chocolates in a microwave-safe bowl and microwave on medium-high, stirring every 30 seconds until melted. Set aside to cool slightly.

In a large-size mixing bowl, with an electric mixer on medium-high speed, beat the butter until light and fluffy. Scrape down the sides of the bowl, reduce the speed to medium, and add half of the confectioners' sugar, cream, vanilla, cayenne, and salt, beating to incorporate. Add the melted chocolates and the rest of the confectioners' sugar, beating on medium-high for 2 to 3 minutes until very smooth and creamy, scraping down the sides of the bowl as needed.

Cupcake Construction: Get out that ice cream scoop (2 to 2¼ inches in diameter) and top each cupcake with frosting. Cupcakes can be refrigerated for up to 3 days in an airtight container, or frozen for 1 month.

If You Like: You can shine them up a bit by taking a butter knife (no serrated edges, please) and pushing the frosting down to about an inch high, flattening the top, and then taking the knife and making a flat 45-degree angled edge all the way around the side of the scoop of frosting.

MIX AND MATCH: Really Hot Dog's Cake with Kick-Off's Vanilla-Spiked Cream Cheese Frosting (page 98)
   Really Hot Dog's Buttercream with Root Beer Float's Root Beer Cake (page 133)

[NOTES]

_____

_____

_____

_____

_____

_____

....

[BUTCH'S BAKING LESSON] You've gotta sift! And you don't need a fancy sifter to do it. Just place a medium-mesh strainer over a bowl that fits, and use a spoon to push the dry ingredients through it. Don't skip this step. No one wants to bite into a lumpy cupcake.

EL DIABLITO

REALLY HOT DOG ::

"We only use full-fat dairy products at the bakery. It's going to taste the best when you don't hold back anything. So go for it!"

BEER RUN ::

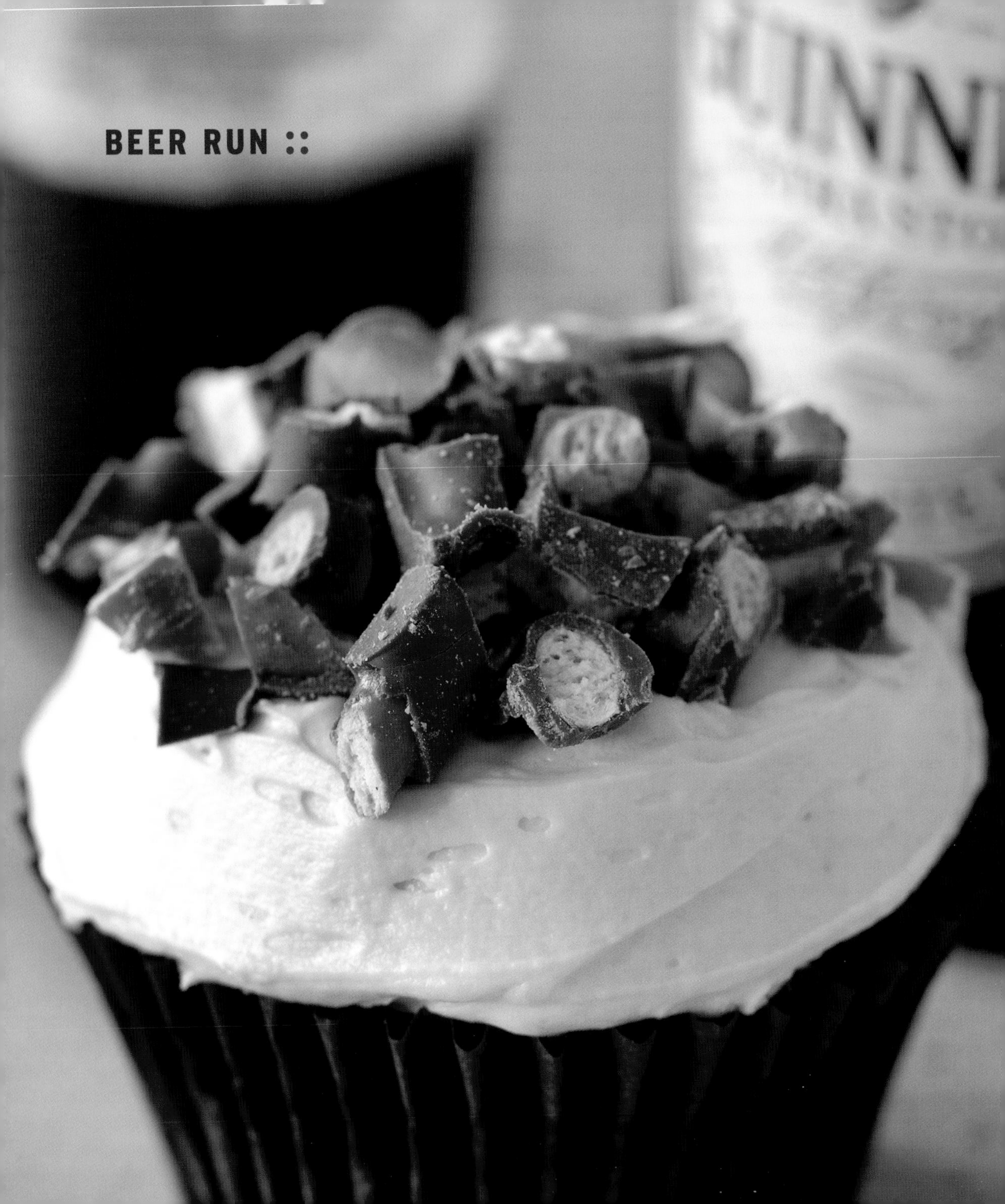

BEER RUN ::

A Chocolate Stout Cupcake with Vanilla Stout Buttercream There's nothing like an ice-cold beer on a hot summer day, or while you're watching your favorite ball game. So we thought, why not make a cupcake with beer? We started with chocolate cake and then added our favorite stout into the mix. Next, we frosted them with our pumped-up creamy vanilla frosting, again with lots of stout, and then topped them with crushed chocolate-covered pretzels. And on that day, a winning combination was born! **[MAKES 12 CUPCAKES]**

INGREDIENT ROSTER:

For the Chocolate Stout Cupcakes:

- 12 tablespoons (1½ sticks) unsalted butter, softened
- ½ cup cocoa powder
- ¾ cup dark stout, such as Guinness, poured and settled before you measure
- 2 large eggs, broken into a small bowl
- ½ cup full-fat sour cream
- 1¼ cups unbleached all-purpose flour
- 1¼ cups sugar
- 1 teaspoon baking soda
- ¼ teaspoon salt

For the Vanilla Stout Buttercream:

- 8 tablespoons (1 stick) unsalted butter, softened
- 3 cups confectioners' sugar, sifted through a strainer
- 3 tablespoons dark stout, such as Guinness, poured and settled before you measure
- ¼ teaspoon pure vanilla extract
- Pinch salt

Topping:

- ¾ cup crushed chocolate-covered pretzels

PLAN OF ATTACK:

Make the Cupcakes: Place a baking rack in the center of the oven and preheat the oven to 350°F. Line two 6-cup jumbo-size muffin pans with liners and set aside.

In a small saucepan over low heat, melt the butter. Remove from the heat, add the cocoa powder, and stir until smooth. Then stir in the stout. You'll think that you have some stout left to drink, but hold your horses! You're going need some for the frosting, too. Set aside to cool, about 10 minutes.

In a medium-size mixing bowl, whisk together the eggs and the sour cream. Add the cooled chocolate mixture, incorporating well. Add the flour, sugar, baking soda, and salt, and whisk until smooth, scraping down the bowl as needed.

Fill each prepared muffin cup with ⅓ cup batter, about ⅔ full. Bake, rotating the pans halfway through, until the tops are just firm to the touch and a tester inserted in the center of a cupcake comes out clean, about 23 minutes. Leave the cupcakes in the pan on a rack to cool for 5 to 10 minutes. Transfer the cupcakes to the wire rack to cool completely before frosting, about 1 hour.

Make the Buttercream: In a medium-size mixing bowl, with an electric mixer on medium-high speed, beat the butter until light and fluffy, about 1 minute. Add the confectioners' sugar, stout, vanilla, and salt into the bowl, and continue to beat until very smooth and creamy, 2 to 3 minutes, scraping down the bowl as needed.

Cupcake Construction: Get out that ice cream scoop (2 to 2¼ inches in diameter) and top each cupcake with a scoop of frosting. Sprinkle each cupcake with a tablespoon of the crushed pretzels. Cupcakes can be refrigerated for up to 3 days in an airtight container, or frozen for 1 month.

If You Like: Before you sprinkle on the pretzels, you can shine the cupcakes up a bit by taking a butter knife (no serrated edges, please) and pushing the frosting down to about an inch high, flattening the top, and then taking the knife and making a flat 45-degree angled edge all the way around the side of the scoop of frosting.

Virgin Beer Run: Substitute your favorite soda for the beer. We like a cola or root beer the best.

MIX AND MATCH: Beer Run's Cake with No-Hitter's Best Chocolate Buttercream (page 89)

Beer Run's Buttercream with Rush Hour's Stout-Spiked Gingerbread (page 61)

[NOTES]

_____

_____

_____

_____

_____

_____

_____

_____

_____

_____

[BUTCH'S BAKING LESSON] You've gotta sift! Always sift your confectioners' sugar. Confectioners' or powdered sugar has cornstarch in it and will be clumpy. If you don't sift it, you will have very lumpy frosting. You can see that in every recipe we remind you to measure it first, and then sift it through a strainer. It's that important! So don't forget.

TRIPLE PLAY ::

A Slammin' Chocolate Cupcake with a Really Rich Chocolate Ganache

Chocolate, chocolate, chocolate. We like to take it to the limit at Butch's. Need a chocolate fix? These will definitely fit the bill. These cupcakes are filled to the brim with chocolate. And then when we thought we added more than enough, we threw in some more for good measure. Plus, this cake is one of those one-pot wonders. You start by using a large (3- to 4-quart) saucepan to melt the butter and chocolate, and then just keep stirring in the rest of the ingredients. Now how hard is that? **[MAKES 12 CUPCAKES]**

INGREDIENT ROSTER:

For the Slammin' Chocolate Cupcakes:

- 8 ounces (2 sticks) unsalted butter
- 1 cup bittersweet chocolate chips (6 ounces)
- 1 cup plus 2 tablespoons sugar
- ¼ cup unsweetened cocoa powder, sifted through a strainer
- 4 large eggs, broken into a small bowl
- 1 tablespoon pure vanilla extract
- 1 cup unbleached all-purpose flour
- 1 teaspoon baking soda
- ¼ teaspoon salt

For the Really Rich Chocolate Ganache:

- 1 cup heavy cream
- 1 tablespoon light corn syrup
  Pinch salt
- 1⅓ cups semisweet chocolate chips (8 ounces)

PLAN OF ATTACK:

Make the Cupcakes: Place a baking rack in the center of the oven and preheat the oven to 350°F. Line two 6-cup jumbo-size muffin pans with liners and set aside.

In a large saucepan over low heat, melt the butter. Remove from the heat and add the chocolate chips, stirring until smooth. Let the mixture cool slightly. Whisk or stir in the sugar and cocoa powder until smooth. Add the beaten eggs and vanilla and combine well. Place a strainer over the pot and sift the flour, baking soda, and salt into the pot, stirring just until the dry ingredients are well incorporated. Make sure to scrape down the sides and the bottom of the pot as needed.

Fill each prepared muffin cup with ⅓ cup batter, about ⅔ full, smoothing the tops. Bake, rotating the pans halfway through, until the tops are just firm to the touch and a tester inserted in the center of a cupcake comes out clean, about 24 minutes. Leave the cupcakes in the pan on a rack to cool for 5 to 10 minutes. Transfer the cupcakes to the wire rack to cool completely before frosting, about 1 hour. They will be a little sunken in the middle. But we want that so that there's more room for the ganache!

Make the Ganache: In a small-size saucepan, heat the cream, corn syrup, and salt until almost boiling. Remove from the heat and add the chocolate chips, stirring until smooth and glossy. Don't worry, keep stirring. The mixture will take some time to become smooth. Cool to room temperature.

Cupcake Construction: Spoon 2 to 3 tablespoons of the ganache on top of each cupcake. Chill to set the ganache, about 1 hour. Cupcakes can be refrigerated for up to 3 days in an airtight container, or frozen for 1 month.

MIX AND MATCH: Triple Play's Cake with 4&10's Peanutty Buttercream (page 105)
Triple Play's Ganache with Old-Fashioned's Extreme Orange Cake (page 151)

[NOTES]

[BUTCH'S BAKING LESSON] Unsweetened cocoa powder is just that. Don't make the mistake of buying hot cocoa mix. And always buy a cocoa with a flavor that you enjoy. That goes for any kind of chocolate bars or chips as well. No two brands taste quite the same. So if you enjoy it straight up, you're going to love it in your cupcakes.

TRIPLE PLAY ::

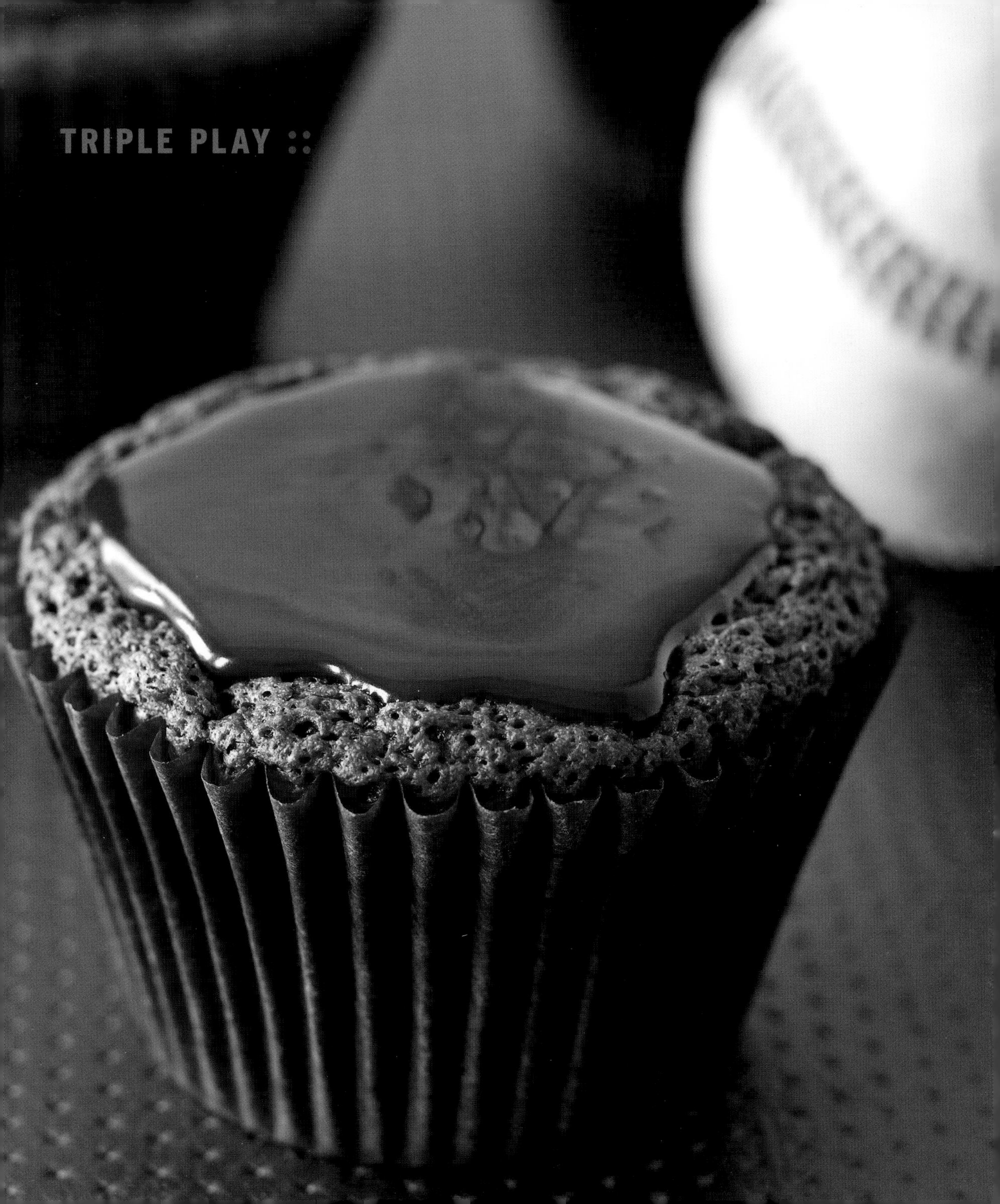

NO-HITTER ::

NO-HITTER ::

A Kick-Ass Yellow Cupcake with the Best Chocolate Buttercream

OK. OK. No liquor, no bacon. But it's still one of the best combinations around—yellow cake with a pile of surprisingly easy rich chocolate buttercream. Now, the cocoa you choose here is going to make all of the difference in this frosting. We switch it up, sometimes using Hershey's—a true American classic—or sometimes using Valrhona—very fancy, but very tasty as well. We can't settle on one choice here, so we're leaving it up to you. Either way, it's a no-hitter in our book. **[MAKES 12 CUPCAKES]**

INGREDIENT ROSTER:

For the Kick-Ass Yellow Cupcakes:

- 1¾ cups cake flour
- 1½ teaspoons baking powder
- ¾ teaspoon salt
- 12 tablespoons (1½ sticks) unsalted butter, softened
- 1½ cups sugar
- 3 large eggs, broken into a small bowl
- 2 teaspoons pure vanilla extract
- ¾ cup whole milk

For the Best Chocolate Buttercream:

- 12 tablespoons (1½ sticks) unsalted butter
- 1 cup unsweetened cocoa powder, Hershey's or Valrhona, sifted through a strainer
- 4¾ cups confectioners' sugar, sifted through a strainer
- ½ cup whole milk
- 2 tablespoons heavy cream
- 2 teaspoons pure vanilla extract
- Pinch salt

PLAN OF ATTACK:

Make the Cupcakes: Place a baking rack in the center of the oven and preheat the oven to 350°F. Line two 6-cup jumbo-size muffin pans with liners and set aside.

Place a strainer over a medium-size mixing bowl and sift together the cake flour, baking powder, and salt. Set aside.

In another medium-size mixing bowl, with an electric mixer on medium-high speed, beat the butter and sugar together until light and fluffy, 2 to 3 minutes. Scrape down the sides of the bowl and add the eggs and vanilla, beating until combined. Add the flour mixture and milk and beat on low speed, just until all the dry ingredients are incorporated, scraping down the sides of the bowl as needed.

Fill each prepared muffin cup with a rounded ⅓ cup batter, about ¾ full. Bake, rotating the pans halfway through, until the tops are just firm to the touch and a tester inserted in the center of a cupcake comes out clean, about 24 minutes. Leave the cupcakes in the pan on a rack to cool for 5 to 10 minutes. Transfer the cupcakes to the wire rack to cool completely before frosting, about 1 hour.

Make the Buttercream: In a medium-size saucepan over low heat, melt the butter. Stir in the cocoa until smooth. Add half of the confectioners' sugar and all of the milk, heavy cream, vanilla, and salt into the pot, beating with a hand mixer until smooth. Scrape down the sides and bottom of the pot, and slowly add the rest of the confectioners' sugar, continuing to beat until very smooth and creamy, 2 to 3 minutes.

Cupcake Construction: Get out that ice cream scoop (2 to 2¼ inches in diameter) and top each cupcake with a generous rounded scoop of frosting. Cupcakes can be refrigerated for up to 3 days in an airtight container, or frozen for 1 month.

If You Like: You can shine the cupcakes up a bit by taking a butter knife (no serrated edges, please) and pushing the frosting down to about an inch high, flattening the top, and then taking the knife and making a flat 45-degree angled edge all the way around the side of the scoop of frosting.

MIX AND MATCH: No-Hitter's Cake with Date Night's Lemon Cream Cheese Frosting (page 143)

   No-Hitter's Buttercream with Coco Loco's Coconut-Swirled Coconut Cake (page 160)

[NOTES]

[BUTCH'S BAKING LESSON] The Eggshell Trick: When you're cracking an egg, the odds are pretty good that if you're not a professional egg cracker, you might have a piece of eggshell fall into your bowl. Crunching on eggshells in your cupcakes is not recommended. But eggshells can be difficult to remove unless you try this trick: Use a piece of the broken eggshell to remove the unwanted piece. Eggshells act like a magnet attracting themselves to each other, and you'll be able to easily remove that pesky piece of shell.

3:
TOUCHDOWN

TAILGATE ::

TAILGATE ::

A Caramel-Filled Cupcake with a Salted Caramel Buttercream At Butch's we love caramel! It's so sweet and smooth. And we like it even better with a salty kick. So we sprinkle some big flakes of salt on the top of each cupcake. But making caramel can be tricky business. It's easy to mess it up. So we've come up with the easiest caramel sauce ever. It's foolproof—works every time. At the bakery, we make the caramel first so it has a little time to cool, and then we poke the warm cupcakes with a skewer and drizzle caramel on top, so it can sink in before we frost them. [MAKES 12 CUPCAKES]

INGREDIENT ROSTER:

For the Caramel Sauce:

12 tablespoons (1½ sticks) unsalted butter

1½ cups firmly packed dark brown sugar

¾ cup firmly packed light brown sugar

¾ cup whole milk

¼ teaspoon salt

For the Caramel Cupcakes:

1¾ cups unbleached all-purpose flour

1½ teaspoons baking powder

¾ teaspoon salt

12 tablespoons (1½ sticks) unsalted butter, softened

1½ cups sugar

3 large eggs, broken into a small bowl

1 teaspoon pure vanilla extract

¾ cup whole milk

For the Salted Caramel Buttercream:

¾ cup reserved caramel sauce

2 cups confectioners' sugar, sifted through a strainer

2 tablespoons unsalted butter, softened

2 tablespoons egg substitute, such as Egg Beaters

¼ teaspoon salt

Topping:

Coarse-grain salt

PLAN OF ATTACK:

Make the Caramel Sauce: In a large-size saucepan over low heat, melt the butter. Add the dark and light brown sugars, milk, and salt, and bring to a boil. Lower the heat to medium and continue to boil for 2 minutes, watching carefully so the mixture doesn't bubble over the pot. Remove from the heat and let cool. Reserve ¾ cup for the caramel buttercream. (You'll have about ⅔ cup left over. Save the caramel in the refrigerator, reheat gently, and drizzle on top of your favorite ice cream.)

Make the Cupcakes: Place a baking rack in the center of the oven and preheat the oven to 350°F. Line two 6-cup jumbo-size muffin pans with liners and set aside.

Place a strainer over a medium-size mixing bowl and sift together the flour, baking powder, and salt. Set aside.

In another medium-size mixing bowl, with an electric mixer on medium-high speed, beat the butter and sugar together until light and fluffy, 2 to 3 minutes. Scrape down the sides of the bowl and add the eggs and vanilla, beating until combined. Add the flour mixture and the milk, beating on low speed, just until all the dry ingredients are incorporated, and scraping down the sides of the bowl as needed.

Fill each prepared muffin cup with a rounded ⅓ cup batter, about ¾ full. Bake, rotating the pans halfway through, until the tops are just firm to the touch and a tester inserted in the center of a cupcake comes out clean, about 24 minutes. Leave the cupcakes in the pan on a rack to cool for 5 to 10 minutes. Transfer the cupcakes to a wire rack and let cool 5 to 10 minutes more.

Make the Buttercream: In a large-size mixing bowl, with an electric mixer on medium-high speed, beat the reserved caramel, confectioners' sugar, butter, egg substitute, and salt until thick and creamy, 2 to 3 minutes, scraping down the sides of the bowl as needed.

Cupcake Construction: To catch drips, place the cupcakes on the wire cooling rack over a foil-lined rimmed baking sheet. While the cupcakes are still warm, poke each one about 15 times with a skewer and drizzle 1½ tablespoons of the warm caramel over the top of each cupcake. Let them cool completely and then spread the tops of each cupcake with 2 rounded tablespoons of frosting. Lightly sprinkle the tops with the salt. Cupcakes can be refrigerated for up to 3 days in an airtight container, or frozen for 1 month.

If You Like: Before sprinkling the salt, you can shine the cupcakes up a bit by taking a butter knife (no serrated edges, please) and pushing the frosting down to about an inch high, flattening the top, and then taking the knife and making a flat 45-degree angled edge all the way around the side of the scoop of frosting.

MIX AND MATCH: Tailgate's Cake and Caramel with Hoo Rah Hoo Rah's Chocolate Drizzle (page 113)

Tailgate's Buttercream with Sweet Mama's Cinnamon Cake (page 146)

....

[BUTCH'S BAKING LESSON] We can't live without eggs in our recipes. And we always crack them into a separate small bowl first, just in case an egg is bad. It doesn't happen very often, but when it does, if you break the eggs directly into the bowl with the other ingredients, you're going to have to fling everything and start over again. So it's best to play it safe, rather than be sorry.

KICK-OFF ::

A Moist Carrot-Pineapple Cupcake with Vanilla-Spiked Cream Cheese Frosting
We all have to eat our veggies, but sometimes we don't want to. Packed with
freshly grated carrots, these cupcakes can kick off your day with a serving of
vegetables in an extremely delicious way. We like to top them with a dollop of
vanilla-spiked cream cheese frosting, but you don't have to; they're delicious
on their own. Who knows, you may even want to have 2 or 3 servings of
vegetables that day. [MAKES 12 CUPCAKES]

INGREDIENT ROSTER:

For the Carrot-Pineapple Cupcakes:

1¼ cups unbleached all-purpose flour

1 teaspoon baking soda

1 teaspoon ground cinnamon

⅛ teaspoon ground nutmeg

½ teaspoon salt

1 cup sugar

½ cup mild vegetable oil

2 large eggs, broken into a small bowl

¼ cup applesauce

1 teaspoon pure vanilla extract

1½ cups peeled and grated carrots (about
3 medium, grated on the large holes
of a box grater)

½ cup raisins

½ cup walnuts, coarsely chopped

¼ cup drained crushed pineapple

For the Vanilla-Spiked Cream Cheese
Frosting:

12 tablespoons (1½ sticks) unsalted
butter, softened

9 ounces cream cheese (three 3-ounce
packages), softened

3 cups confectioners' sugar, sifted
through a strainer

1½ tablespoons heavy cream

1½ teaspoons pure vanilla extract

Topping: (optional)

¾ cup chopped walnuts

PLAN OF ATTACK:

Make the Cupcakes: Place a baking rack in the center of the oven and preheat the oven to 350°F. Line two 6-cup jumbo-size muffin pans with liners and set aside.

Place a strainer over a medium-size mixing bowl and sift together the flour, baking soda, cinnamon, nutmeg, and salt. Set aside.

In another medium-size mixing bowl, whisk the sugar, oil, eggs, applesauce, and vanilla together until creamy. Switch to a large spoon and stir in the flour mixture, mixing just to combine. Stir in the carrots, raisins, walnuts, and pineapple until well coated with batter. Fill each prepared muffin cup with $\frac{1}{3}$ cup batter, about $\frac{2}{3}$ full. Bake, rotating the pans halfway through, until the tops are just firm to the touch and a tester inserted in the center of a cupcake comes out clean, about 25 minutes. Leave the cupcakes in the pan on a rack to cool for 5 to 10 minutes. Transfer the cupcakes to the wire rack to cool completely before frosting, about 1 hour.

Make the Frosting: In a large-size mixing bowl, with a mixer on medium-high speed, beat the butter and the cream cheese until light and fluffy; do not overbeat. Add half of the confectioners' sugar, the heavy cream, and vanilla and beat until smooth. Scrape down the bowl and add the rest of the confectioners' sugar. Continue to beat on medium-high speed until thick and creamy, 2 to 3 minutes, scraping down the sides of the bowl as needed.

Cupcake Construction: Get out that ice cream scoop (2 to 2$\frac{1}{4}$ inches in diameter) and top each cupcake with a generous rounded scoop of frosting. Sprinkle 1 tablespoon chopped walnuts on the top of each cupcake, if desired. Cupcakes can be refrigerated for up to 3 days in an airtight container, or frozen for 1 month.

If You Like: Before you sprinkle on the walnuts, you can shine the cupcakes up a bit by taking a butter knife (no serrated edges, please) and pushing the frosting down to about an inch high, flattening the top, and then taking the knife and making a flat 45-degree angled edge all the way around the side of the scoop of frosting.

MIX AND MATCH: Kick-Off's Cake with Rush Hour's Ginger Buttercream (page 61) Kick-Off's Frosting with Defense Defense's Red Velvet Cake (page 108)

[NOTES]

_____

_____

_____

_____

_____

_____

_____

_____

_____

_____

_____

_____

[BUTCH'S BAKING LESSON] These have some applesauce in them to reduce the amount of oil that you would typically find in carrot cakes. We all work out here, but why add extra calories if you don't need to? So whenever you see a lot of oil in a baking recipe, you can probably cut that amount by $\frac{1}{3}$ and substitute applesauce instead. Plus, try to get organic carrots—they're sweeter.

KICK-OFF ::

"Baking is a science! So make sure you always measure your ingredients correctly. Mess that up and you're not going to get the results you're expecting!"

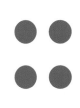

4&10 ::

A Chocolate Chip Banana Cupcake topped with Peanutty Buttercream

This one came from my cousin Gary's wife, Penny. And I have to say that it has been a family favorite for quite awhile now. The smooth peanutty buttercream on top of this tasty banana cupcake studded with chocolate chips will get everybody's attention. Cousin Gary was the police chief in Burlington, Vermont, for many years, and when he would bring these down to the station, within minutes—and I mean minutes—not a crumb was left. They pretty much inhaled them—a touchdown every single time. Thanks Penny!

[MAKES 12 CUPCAKES]

INGREDIENT ROSTER:

For the Chocolate Chip Banana Cupcakes:

- 1¾ cups cake flour
- 1 teaspoon baking powder
- ½ teaspoon baking soda
- ½ teaspoon salt
- 8 tablespoons (1 stick) unsalted butter, softened
- ½ cup sugar
- ½ cup firmly packed light brown sugar
- 2 large eggs, broken into a small bowl
- ½ teaspoon pure vanilla extract
- ½ cup buttermilk
- 1 cup mashed very ripe banana, about 3 medium
- 1 cup semisweet chocolate chips, tossed in 1 teaspoon cake flour

For the Peanutty Buttercream:

- 6 tablespoons (¾ stick) unsalted butter, softened
- 1 cup creamy peanut butter (not freshly ground)
- 1⅓ cups confectioners' sugar, sifted through a strainer
- 1½ teaspoons pure vanilla extract
- ⅓ cup heavy cream
- Pinch salt

Topping: (optional)

- ¾ cup honey-roasted peanuts, roughly chopped

PLAN OF ATTACK:

Make the Cupcakes: Place a baking rack in the center of the oven and preheat the oven to 350°F. Line two 6-cup jumbo-size muffin pans with liners and set aside.

Place a strainer over a medium-size mixing bowl and sift together the cake flour, baking powder, baking soda, and salt. Set aside.

In another medium-size mixing bowl, with an electric mixer on medium-high speed, beat the butter, sugar, and brown sugar together until well combined, 2 to 3 minutes. Scrape down the sides of the bowl and add the eggs and vanilla, beating until combined. Add the flour mixture and the buttermilk and beat on low speed just until all the dry ingredients are incorporated, scraping down the sides of the bowl as needed. Stir in the mashed banana, combining well, and then the chocolate chips.

Fill each prepared muffin cup with a rounded ⅓ cup batter, about ¾ full. Bake, rotating the pans halfway through, until the tops are just firm to the touch and a tester inserted in the center of a cupcake comes out clean, about 24 minutes. Leave the cupcakes in the pan on a rack to cool for 5 to 10 minutes. Transfer the cupcakes to the wire rack to cool completely before frosting, about 1 hour.

Make the Buttercream: In a large-size mixing bowl, with an electric mixer on medium-high speed, beat the butter and peanut butter together until creamy. Scrape down the sides of the bowl, reduce the speed to medium, and add the confectioners' sugar, vanilla, heavy cream, and salt, beating on medium-high speed for 2 to 3 minutes until very smooth and creamy, scraping down the sides of the bowl as needed.

Cupcake Construction: Top each cupcake with a heaping tablespoon of the frosting, and using a butter knife or small offset spatula, smooth the frosting on the top of each cupcake. Sprinkle the tops with 1 tablespoon of the peanuts, if desired. Cupcakes can be refrigerated for up to 3 days in an airtight container, or frozen for 1 month.

MIX AND MATCH: 4&10's Cake with Home Run's Banana Buttercream (page 71)
4&10's Buttercream with Driller's Maple Cake (page 46)

[NOTES]

_____

_____

_____

_____

_____

_____

_____

_____

_____

_____

_____

_____

_____

_____

[BUTCH'S BAKING LESSON] Bananas on the ready! You may have a craving for these cupcakes and no ripe bananas to be found. So when you have overripe bananas around, freeze them in their peels. Then, when you need them, just defrost and mash them up. You'll never be without another banana for this recipe again.

DEFENSE DEFENSE ::

A Red Velvet Cupcake with Jack Daniel's Cream Cheese Frosting

Red Velvet is hot right now. And at Butch's we have one of the best red velvet cupcakes going. Of course ours are big and beautiful, but we couldn't stop there. We just had to jazz up the cream cheese frosting. So why not a jigger of Jack Daniel's? **[MAKES 12 CUPCAKES]**

INGREDIENT ROSTER:

For the Red Velvet Cupcakes:

- 1¾ cups cake flour
- 1 tablespoon unsweetened cocoa powder
- 1½ teaspoons baking soda
- ½ teaspoon salt
- 1 cup mild vegetable oil
- 1¼ cups sugar
- 2 large eggs, broken into a small bowl
- 1 tablespoon red liquid food color
- 2 teaspoons pure vanilla extract
- ½ teaspoon white vinegar
- ¾ cup well-shaken buttermilk

For the Jack Daniel's Cream Cheese Frosting:

- 8 tablespoons (1 stick) unsalted butter, softened
- 4 ounces cream cheese, softened
- 3½ cups confectioners' sugar, sifted through a strainer
- 3 tablespoons Jack Daniel's
- ¼ teaspoon salt

PLAN OF ATTACK:

Make the Cupcakes: Place a baking rack in the center of the oven and preheat the oven to 350°F. Line two 6-cup jumbo-size muffin pans with liners and set aside.

Place a strainer over a medium-size mixing bowl and sift together the cake flour, cocoa, baking soda, and salt. Set aside.

In a medium-size mixing bowl, whisk the oil and sugar together until well combined. Add the eggs, red food color, vanilla, and white vinegar and whisk until smooth and creamy. Add the flour mixture and buttermilk and continue to stir or beat just until all the dry ingredients are incorporated, scraping down the sides of the bowl as needed.

Fill each of the prepared muffin cups with a rounded $\frac{1}{3}$ cup batter, about $\frac{3}{4}$ full. Bake, rotating the pans halfway through, until the tops are just firm to the touch and a tester inserted in the center of a cupcake comes out clean, about 23 minutes. Leave the cupcakes in the pan on a rack to cool for 5 to 10 minutes. Transfer the cupcakes to the wire rack to cool completely before frosting, about 1 hour.

Make the Frosting: In a large-size mixing bowl with an electric mixer on medium-high speed, beat the butter and cream cheese until light and fluffy. Scrape down the sides of the bowl, reduce the speed to medium, and add half of the confectioners' sugar, the Jack Daniel's, and salt, beating to incorporate. Add the rest of the confectioners' sugar, beating on medium-high for 2 to 3 minutes until very smooth and creamy, scraping down the sides of the bowl as needed.

Cupcake Construction: Get out that ice cream scoop (2 to $2\frac{1}{4}$ inches in diameter) and top each cupcake with a generous rounded scoop of frosting. Cupcakes can be refrigerated for up to 3 days in an airtight container, or frozen for 1 month.

If You Like: You can shine them up a bit by taking a butter knife (no serrated edges, please) and pushing the frosting down to about an inch high, flattening the top, and then taking the knife and making a flat 45-degree angled edge all the way around the side of the scoop of frosting.

Virgin Defense Defense: In the frosting, substitute 3 tablespoons heavy cream for the Jack Daniel's.

MIX AND MATCH: Defense Defense's Cake with Kick-Off's Vanilla-Spiked Cream Cheese Frosting (page 98)

Defense Defense's Frosting with Old-Fashioned's Extreme Orange Cake (page 151)

[NOTES]

_____

_____

_____

_____

_____

_____

_____

_____

_____

_____

[BUTCH'S BAKING LESSON] Full-Fat vs. Low- and No-Fat: Come on here. This is dessert, a treat. Why play around with low-fat and no-fat dairy? We only use full-fat dairy products at the bakery. It's going to taste the best when you don't hold back anything. So go for it!

HOO RAH HOO RAH! ::

HOO RAH HOO RAH! ::

A Black-Bottom Devil's Food Cupcake filled with Chocolate Chip Cheesecake and topped with a big Chocolate Drizzle It'll be like you're in the stands screaming Hoo Rah when you bite into one of these. Cheesecake inside a devil's food cupcake? How could we go wrong? Then we couldn't help ourselves. We had to gild the lily and top them with some more chocolate. HOO RAH! [MAKES 12 CUPCAKES]

INGREDIENT ROSTER:

For the Chocolate Chip Cheesecake Filling:

- 1 large egg, broken into a small bowl
- 8 ounces cream cheese, softened
- ⅓ cup firmly packed light brown sugar
- 1 teaspoon pure vanilla extract
- ¾ cup semisweet chocolate chips

For the Black-Bottom Devil's Food Cupcakes:

- ⅓ cup mild vegetable oil
- 1 cup firmly packed light brown sugar
- 1 cup water
- 1 tablespoon white vinegar
- 1 tablespoon pure vanilla extract
- 1½ cups unbleached all-purpose flour
- ½ cup unsweetened cocoa powder
- 1 teaspoon baking soda
- ½ teaspoon salt

For the Chocolate Drizzle:

- ¼ cup heavy cream
- 1 teaspoon light corn syrup
- ½ cup semisweet chocolate chips

PLAN OF ATTACK:

Place a baking rack in the center of the oven and preheat the oven to 350°F. Line two 6-cup jumbo-size muffin pans with liners and set aside.

Make the Filling: In a small mixing bowl, with an electric mixer on medium speed, beat together the egg, cream cheese, brown sugar, and vanilla until smooth. Stir in the chips and set aside.

Make the Cupcakes: In a medium-size mixing bowl, whisk together the oil, brown sugar, water, vinegar, and vanilla until the brown sugar is dissolved. Place a strainer over the mixing bowl and sift the flour, cocoa powder, baking soda, and salt over the wet ingredients. Mix just until all the dry ingredients are incorporated.

Fill each prepared muffin cup with ¼ cup batter, about ½ full, and top the center of each cupcake with 2 tablespoons of the cheesecake filling. Bake, rotating the pans halfway through, until the cake and filling are just firm to the touch, about 25 minutes. Leave the cupcakes in the pan on a rack to cool for 5 to 10 minutes. Transfer the cupcakes to the wire rack to cool completely before drizzling with chocolate, about 1 hour.

Make the Chocolate Drizzle: In a small saucepan, heat the cream and corn syrup until very hot but not boiling. Remove from the heat, and stir in the chips until smooth. Let cool slightly.

Cupcake Construction: Using a measuring tablespoon, thickly drizzle 1 tablespoon of the chocolate drizzle over each cupcake. Cupcakes can be refrigerated for up to 3 days in an airtight container, or frozen for 1 month.

MIX AND MATCH: Hoo Rah Hoo Rah's Cake and Filling with Triple Play's Really Rich Chocolate Ganache (page 84)

Hoo Rah Hoo Rah's Drizzle with 4&10's Chocolate Chip Banana Cake (page 105)

[BUTCH'S BAKING LESSON] Did you know that oil can go bad? Well, it can go rancid, which is not something you want to use in your cupcakes. So keep the oil refrigerated, and give it a sniff before you use it. You'll know if it went bad or not, trust us.

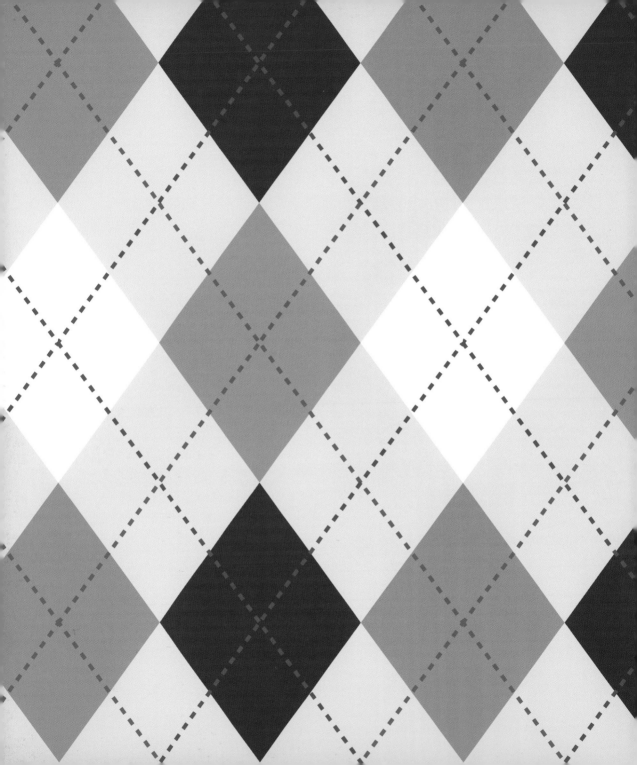

4:

BARBECUE SEASON

MOJITO ::

MOJITO ::

A Rum-Soaked Lime Cupcake with a Muddled Minty Lime Cream Cheese Frosting OK, it's time for a little history lesson. The mojito (moh-HEE-toh) is one of Cuba's oldest cocktails, dating back to the late 1500's when Sir Francis Drake and his pirates tried and failed to invade Havana for its gold. His cohort Richard Drake is said to have invented it during the invasion—now that's old and manly. The name originates from the African word "mojo," which means to place a little spell on you. These cupcakes, with a kick of lime and rum in the cake and topped with our minty lime cream cheese frosting, will certainly put you into a trance. [MAKES 12 CUPCAKES]

INGREDIENT ROSTER:

For the Lime Cupcakes:

- 1½ cups plus 2 tablespoons cake flour
- 1½ teaspoons baking powder
- ½ teaspoon salt
- 12 tablespoons (1½ sticks) unsalted butter, softened
- 1 cup plus 2 tablespoons sugar
- 2 large eggs, broken into a small bowl
- ¼ cup fresh lime juice (from 3 to 4 limes)
- 1 tablespoon grated lime zest
- 1 teaspoon pure vanilla extract
- ⅓ cup heavy cream

For the Muddled Minty Lime Cream Cheese Frosting:

- 8 ounces cream cheese, softened

- 12 tablespoons (1½ sticks) unsalted butter, softened
- 4 cups confectioners' sugar, sifted through a strainer
- ¼ cup whole milk
- 1 teaspoon peppermint extract
- 2 teaspoons grated lime zest

For the Soaking Liquid:

- ¼ to ½ cup dark rum, such as Mount Gay

Topping: (optional)

Lime Sawdust (recipe follows)

PLAN OF ATTACK:

Make the Cupcakes: Place a baking rack in the center of the oven and preheat the oven to 350°F. Line two 6-cup jumbo-size muffin pans with liners and set aside.

Place a strainer over a medium-size mixing bowl and sift together the cake flour, baking powder, and salt. Set aside.

In another medium-size mixing bowl, with an electric mixer on medium-high speed, beat the butter and sugar together until light and fluffy. Scrape down the bowl and add the eggs, lime juice, zest, and vanilla, mixing until well combined. It will look curdled—not a problem. Add the flour mixture and the cream and mix just until all of the dry ingredients are incorporated, scraping the bowl as needed. The batter will be thick.

Fill each prepared muffin cup with ⅓ cup batter, about ⅔ full, smoothing the tops. Bake, rotating the pans halfway through, until the tops are just firm to the touch and a tester inserted in the center of a cupcake comes out clean, about 24 minutes. Leave the cupcakes in the pan on a rack to cool for 5 to 10 minutes. Transfer the cupcakes to the wire rack to cool completely before frosting, about 1 hour.

Make the Frosting: In a large-size mixing bowl, beat the cream cheese and the butter until light and fluffy. Scrape down the bowl and add half of the confectioners' sugar and beat until smooth. Add the rest of the confectioners' sugar, the milk, peppermint extract, and lime zest, continuing to beat on medium-high speed until thick and creamy, 2 to 3 minutes, scraping down the sides of the bowl as needed.

Cupcake Construction: Using a wooden skewer, poke about 15 holes in the top of each cupcake and slowly spoon 1 to 2 teaspoons of the rum over the top of each cupcake. Let them sit for 15 minutes to allow the rum to be absorbed. Now get out that ice cream scoop (2 to 2¼ inches in diameter) and top each cupcake with a scoop of the frosting. Sprinkle the tops with ¼ to ½ teaspoon of the lime sawdust, if desired. Cupcakes can be refrigerated for up to 3 days in an airtight container, or frozen for 1 month.

If You Like: Before sprinkling the tops, you can shine the cupcakes up a bit by taking a butter knife (no serrated edges, please) and pushing the frosting down to about an inch high, flattening the top, and then taking the knife and making a flat 45-degree angled edge all the way around the side of the scoop of frosting.

Virgin Mojito: Skip soaking the cupcakes with rum.

Lime Sawdust: In a small bowl, mix together 2 tablespoons sugar and ½ teaspoon grated lime zest.

MIX AND MATCH: Mojito's Cake with Date Night's Lemon Cream Cheese Frosting (page 143)
   Mojito's Frosting with Rum & Coke's Rum Cake (page 122)

[NOTES]

_____

_____

_____

_____

_____

_____

[BUTCH'S BAKING LESSON] You will need a lot of lime juice and zest for this recipe, from 3 or 4 limes. So do it all at once. Pressing down and rolling the limes on the counter will break up some of their fibers and make them juicier. And don't forget to grate the limes' zest first before you cut them.

RUM & COKE ::

A Rum-Soaked Rum Cupcake with The Real Thing Cola Buttercream

Rum and Coke is truly the pause that refreshes. We've overloaded the cake with rum and topped it with a buttercream made with real cola syrup. Close your eyes, bite into this one, and you'll think you're sittin' in a beach chair on the Jersey shore on a hot summer's day. **[MAKES 12 CUPCAKES]**

INGREDIENT ROSTER:

For the Rum Cupcakes:

- 2 cups cake flour
- 1 teaspoon baking powder
- ¾ teaspoon baking soda
- ½ teaspoon salt
- 8 tablespoons (1 stick) unsalted butter, softened
- 1 cup sugar
- 2 large eggs, broken into a small bowl
- 2 teaspoons pure vanilla extract
- ½ cup well shaken buttermilk
- ½ cup dark rum, such as Mount Gay

For The Real Thing Cola Buttercream:

- 12 tablespoons (1½ sticks) unsalted butter, softened
- 4½ cups confectioners' sugar, sifted through a strainer
- 2½ tablespoons Cola Syrup, such as the Vermont Country Store brand
- 3 tablespoons whole milk

For the Soaking Liquid:

- ¼ cup dark rum, such as Mount Gay

PLAN OF ATTACK:

Make the Cupcakes: Place a baking rack in the center of the oven and preheat the oven to 350°F. Line two 6-cup jumbo-size muffin pans with liners and set aside.

Place a strainer over a medium-size mixing bowl, and sift together the cake flour, baking powder, baking soda, and salt. Set aside.

In another medium-size mixing bowl, with an electric mixer on medium-high speed, beat the butter and sugar together until light and fluffy. Scrape down the sides of the bowl, and add the eggs and vanilla, mixing until well combined. Add about half of the flour mixture and all of the buttermilk and mix just until all the dry ingredients are incorporated. Add the rest of the flour mixture and the rum, and mix just to combine, scraping down the sides of the bowl as needed.

Fill each prepared muffin cup with a rounded ⅓ cup batter, about ¾ full, smoothing the tops. Bake, rotating the pans halfway through, until the tops are just firm to the touch and a tester inserted in the center of a cupcake comes out clean, about 23 minutes. Leave the cupcakes in the pan on a rack to cool for 5 to 10 minutes. Transfer the cupcakes to the wire rack to cool completely before frosting, about 1 hour.

Make the Buttercream: In a large-size mixing bowl, with an electric mixer on medium-high speed, beat the butter until light and fluffy. Scrape down the sides of the bowl and add half of the confectioners' sugar, the cola syrup, and milk, beating to combine. Add the rest of the confectioners' sugar and continue to beat on medium-high speed until thick and creamy, 2 to 3 minutes more, scraping down the sides of the bowl as needed.

Cupcake Construction: Slowly spoon 1 to 1½ tablespoons of the rum over the top of each cupcake. Let them sit for 10 minutes to allow the rum to be absorbed. Then get out that ice cream scoop (2 to 2¼ inches in diameter) and top each cupcake with a generous rounded scoop of frosting. Cupcakes can be refrigerated for up to 3 days in an airtight container, or frozen for 1 month.

If You Like: You can shine them up a bit by taking a butter knife (no serrated edges, please) and pushing the frosting down to about an inch high, flattening the top, and then taking the knife and making a flat 45-degree angled edge all the way around the side of the scoop of frosting.

Virgin No Rum & Coke: In the cake, substitute another ½ cup buttermilk for the rum.

MIX AND MATCH: Rum & Coke's Cake with Big Papi's White Chocolate–Rum Raisin Buttercream (page 127)

Rum and Coke's Buttercream with Side Car's Lip-Puckering Lemon Cake (page 157)

[NOTES]

_____

_____

_____

_____

_____

_____

_____

_____

_____

[BUTCH'S BAKING LESSON] Don't have any buttermilk? No worries! Just stir 1 tablespoon fresh lemon juice or white vinegar into 1 cup of whole milk and let stand for 5 minutes—buttermilk!

RUM & COKE ::

BIG PAPI ::

BIG PAPI ::

Dad's Spiced-Up Cupcake filled and topped with White Chocolate–Rum Raisin Buttercream When we decided to add a spice cupcake to the menu at Butch's, we knew that we wanted it to be really spicy. So you'll find a big hit of cinnamon, allspice, and nutmeg in these guys. Matching a frosting was a no-brainer here. We soak raisins in lots of rum and mix them into a rum-flavored white chocolate buttercream—the perfect match! For this recipe we like Mount Gay Sugar Cane Rum, but any dark rum will do the trick

[MAKES 12 CUPCAKES]

INGREDIENT ROSTER:

For the Rum Raisins:

- ¾ cup raisins
- ½ cup dark rum, such as Mount Gay

For Dad's Spiced-Up Cupcakes:

- 1¼ cups unbleached all-purpose flour
- 1 teaspoon baking powder
- ¾ teaspoon baking soda
- 1½ teaspoons ground cinnamon
- ¾ teaspoon allspice
- ¼ teaspoon ground nutmeg
- ½ teaspoon salt
- 8 tablespoons (1 stick) unsalted butter, softened
- 1 cup firmly packed light brown sugar
- 3 large eggs, broken into a small bowl
- ¾ cup well-shaken buttermilk

For the White Chocolate–Rum Raisin Buttercream:

- 12 tablespoons (1½ sticks) unsalted butter, softened
- 4 cups confectioners' sugar, sifted through a strainer
- 3 tablespoons heavy cream
- 2 tablespoons dark rum, reserved from the rum raisins
- 1½ teaspoons pure vanilla extract
- ⅛ teaspoon salt
- 1½ cups white chocolate chips, melted and cooled slightly

PLAN OF ATTACK:

Make the Rum Raisins: In a small bowl, combine the raisins and rum and let soak for 20 to 30 minutes. Drain the raisins very, very well, reserving 2 tablespoons of the rum for the buttercream.

Make the Cupcakes: Place a baking rack in the center of the oven and preheat the oven to 350°F. Line two 6-cup jumbo-size muffin pans with liners and set aside.

Place a strainer over a medium-size mixing bowl and sift together the flour, baking powder, baking soda, cinnamon, allspice, nutmeg, and salt. Set aside.

In another medium-size mixing bowl, with an electric mixer on medium-high speed, beat the butter and brown sugar together until well combined, 2 to 3 minutes. Scrape down the sides of the bowl, and add the eggs, beating until combined. Add about half of the flour mixture and the buttermilk, and mix just until all the dry ingredients are incorporated. Add the rest of the flour mixture and mix just until well combined, scraping down the sides of the bowl as needed.

Fill each prepared muffin cup with a rounded ⅓ cup batter, about ¾ full. Bake, rotating the pans halfway through, until the tops are just firm to the touch and a tester inserted in the center of the cupcake comes out clean, about 23 minutes. Leave the cupcakes in the pan on a rack to cool for 5 to 10 minutes. Transfer the cupcakes to the wire rack to cool completely before filling and frosting, about 1 hour.

Make the Buttercream: In a large-size mixing bowl, with an electric mixer on medium-high speed, beat the butter until light and fluffy. Scrape down the sides of the bowl, and add half of the confectioners' sugar, the cream, rum, vanilla, and salt, beating on medium-high to combine. Add the rest of the confectioners' sugar, beating until smooth. Add the melted white chocolate and continue to beat for 2 to 3 minutes until very smooth and creamy, scraping down the sides of the bowl as needed.

Rum Raisin Filling: Remove 1 cup of the frosting and stir in ½ cup of the rum raisins. (Remember to drain them very well.) Reserve the rest to garnish the tops of the cupcakes.

Cupcake Construction: With a small knife or melon baller, carve a 2 x 2-inch hole in the top of each cupcake. Fill with 1 to 2 tablespoons of the rum raisin filling. Then get out that ice cream scoop (2 to 2¼ inches in diameter), top each cupcake with frosting, and sprinkle a few of the reserved raisins on top of the center of each cupcake. Cupcakes can be refrigerated for up to 3 days in an airtight container, or frozen for 1 month.

If You Like: Before topping with the raisins, you can shine the cupcakes up a bit by taking a butter knife (no serrated edges, please) and pushing the frosting down to about an inch high, flattening the top, and then taking the knife and making a flat 45-degree angled edge all the way around the side of the scoop of frosting.

Virgin Big Papi: Soak the raisins in ½ cup warm water, and for the frosting, substitute 2 tablespoons heavy cream for the rum.

MIX AND MATCH: Big Papi's Cake with Rush Hour's Ginger Buttercream (page 61)
Big Papi's Buttercream with Rum & Coke's Rum Cake (page 122)

....

[BUTCH'S BAKING LESSON] Melting Chocolate: A lot of people will tell you that you should melt chocolate in a double boiler over simmering water, but you always risk getting a little water in the chocolate, which could make that expensive chocolate seize up. At Butch's, we prefer to melt the chocolate in a very heavy saucepan over very low heat, stirring constantly until smooth. Very low heat is key here, so that you don't burn the chocolate. You could also melt it in the microwave, not on the highest setting, checking and stirring every 30 seconds until smooth.

"At Butch's we don't use anything other than the real thing—nothing imitation here. Promise us you'll do that too!"

ROOT BEER FLOAT ::

ROOT BEER FLOAT ::

A Root Beer Cupcake with Double-Strength Vanilla–Root Beer Buttercream

There's nothing like an ice-cold root beer in a frosty mug to quench your thirst. Root beer has a very distinctive flavor, and it took us a couple of tries to get it right in this cupcake. We tried putting a whole bottle of it into this recipe, even boiled the soda down to concentrate the flavor, but it just wasn't root-beery enough. So this is one of the rare times that you're going to have to search out an unusual ingredient–root beer extract. That's the only way you'll get that kick of genuine root beer in the cupcake and the buttercream!

[MAKES 12 CUPCAKES]

INGREDIENT ROSTER:

For the Root Beer Cupcakes:

- 1½ cups cake flour
- 2 teaspoons baking powder
- ½ teaspoon salt
- 8 tablespoons (1 stick) unsalted butter, softened
- ¾ cup sugar
- 2 large eggs, broken into a small bowl
- 2 teaspoons root beer extract, such as Green Mountain Flavors or Zatarain's
- ¼ cup root beer (not diet), settled and then poured
- ¼ cup heavy cream

For the Double-Strength Vanilla–Root Beer Buttercream:

- 12 ounces (3 sticks) unsalted butter, softened
- 3½ cups confectioners' sugar, sifted through a strainer
- 1½ tablespoons heavy cream
- 2¼ teaspoons root beer extract
- 2 teaspoons pure vanilla extract

Topping: (optional)

- 1 tablespoon finely crushed root beer candies

PLAN OF ATTACK:

Make the Cupcakes: Place a baking rack in the center of the oven and preheat the oven to 350°F. Line two 6-cup jumbo-size muffin pans with liners and set aside.

Place a strainer over a medium-size mixing bowl and sift together the cake flour, baking powder, and salt. Set aside.

In another medium-size mixing bowl, with an electric mixer on medium-high speed, beat the butter and sugar together until light and fluffy, 2 to 3 minutes. Scrape down the sides of the bowl, and add the eggs and root beer extract, beating until combined. Add the flour mixture, root beer, and heavy cream, and beat on low speed just until all the dry ingredients are incorporated, scraping down the sides of the bowl as needed.

Fill each prepared muffin cup with ¼ cup batter, about ½ full. Bake, rotating the pans halfway through, until the tops are just firm to the touch and a tester inserted in the center of a cupcake comes out clean, about 22 minutes. Leave the cupcakes in the pan on a rack to cool for 5 to 10 minutes. Transfer the cupcakes to the wire rack to cool completely before frosting, about 1 hour.

Make the Buttercream: In a large-size mixing bowl, with an electric mixer on medium-high speed, beat the butter until light and fluffy. Scrape down the sides of the bowl, reduce the speed to medium, and add half of the confectioners' sugar, the heavy cream, root beer extract, and vanilla extract, beating to incorporate. Add the rest of the confectioners' sugar, beating on medium-high speed for 2 to 3 minutes until very smooth and creamy, scraping down the sides of the bowl as needed.

Cupcake Construction: Get out that ice cream scoop (2 to 2¼ inches in diameter) and top each cupcake with a generous rounded scoop of frosting. Sprinkle on ¼ teaspoon of the crushed root beer candies, if desired. Cupcakes can be refrigerated for up to 3 days in an airtight container, or frozen for 1 month.

If You Like: Before you sprinkle on the root beer candies, you can shine the cupcakes up a bit by taking a butter knife (no serrated edges, please) and pushing the frosting down to about an inch high, flattening the top, and then taking the knife and making a flat 45-degree angled edge all the way around the side of the scoop of frosting.

MIX AND MATCH: Root Beer Float's Cake with No-Hitter's Best Chocolate Buttercream (page 89)

Root Beer Float's Buttercream with Triple Play's Slammin' Chocolate Cake (page 84)

[NOTES]

_____

_____

_____

_____

_____

_____

_____

_____

_____

[BUTCH'S BAKING LESSON] The Oven (Part 1): Just because your oven tells you that it has reached a temperature of 350°F doesn't mean that it really has. As a matter of fact, most ovens, even those high-end ones, are not always very accurate. Plus, the signals that tell you that it has come up to temperature aren't always accurate either. It takes a full 15 to 20 minutes for your oven to reach 350°F. So what's a guy to do? Buy a reliable oven thermometer for your oven, and you'll always know the exact temperature inside your oven—and when it's hot enough to begin baking your cupcakes.

CAMP OUT ::

A Graham Cracker and Milk Chocolate–Swirled Vanilla-Cinnamon Cupcake topped with S'mores Topping Remember when you were a kid and you stood in front of the outdoor grill roasting marshmallows on a stick? And then you'd stick those gooey, toasted pillows between 2 pieces of graham cracker along with a large square of milk chocolate? Heaven. Well, this is as close to that as you're going to get in a cupcake. We make a graham cracker filling that we layer in our cinnamon-scented cupcake with a square of milk chocolate. Then we top it with another square of milk chocolate and a lot of gooey toasted marshmallow. You'll be a kid all over again.

If you can, eat them warm, while the marshmallow is still gooey and the chocolate is still melted, but they're great when they're completely cooled, too.

[MAKES 12 CUPCAKES]

INGREDIENT ROSTER:

For the Graham Cracker and Milk Chocolate Swirl:

- 3 2½ x 5-inch graham crackers
- ¼ cup firmly packed light brown sugar
- 1 tablespoon unsalted butter, softened
- ½ teaspoon pure vanilla extract
- ⅛ teaspoon salt
- 2 1.55-ounce milk chocolate bars, such as Hershey's, broken into 1½-inch squares

For the Vanilla-Cinnamon Cupcakes:

- 1½ cups unbleached all-purpose flour
- 2½ teaspoons baking powder
- 1 teaspoon salt
- ½ teaspoon ground cinnamon

- 10 tablespoons (1¼ sticks) unsalted butter, softened
- 1 cup firmly packed light brown sugar
- 2 large eggs, broken into a small bowl
- 1 tablespoon pure vanilla extract
- ½ cup whole milk
- ½ cup heavy cream

S'more's Topping:

- 2 1.55-ounce milk chocolate bars, such as Hershey's, broken into 1½-inch squares
- 6 giant marshmallows, such as Campfire Giant Roasters, sliced in half lengthwise, or 3 cups mini marshmallows

PLAN OF ATTACK:

Make the Graham Cracker and Milk Chocolate Swirl: In the bowl of a food processor, combine all of the ingredients and process into fine crumbs, scraping down the sides of the work bowl as needed. Transfer to a small bowl. (Alternatively, for the graham crackers, you could crush the crackers in a resealable plastic bag and stir in the other ingredients until combined.)

Make the Cupcakes: Place a baking rack in the center of the oven and preheat the oven to 350°F. Line two 6-cup jumbo-size muffin pans with liners and set aside.

Place a strainer over a medium-size mixing bowl and sift together the flour, baking powder, salt, and cinnamon. Set aside.

In another medium-size mixing bowl, with an electric mixer on medium-high speed, beat the butter and brown sugar together until light and fluffy. Add the eggs and vanilla, and mix until well combined, scraping down the sides of the bowl. Add the flour mixture, milk, and cream, mixing just until all the dry ingredients are incorporated, scraping down the sides of the bowl as needed. Batter will be thick.

Spread one heaping tablespoon of batter in the bottom of each prepared muffin cup. Evenly sprinkle one level tablespoon of the graham cracker swirl on top of the batter, and then place one 1½-inch square of the milk chocolate on top. Cover with one more heaping tablespoon of batter, and smooth the tops. Bake, rotating the pans halfway through, until the tops are just firm to the touch, about 25 minutes. (A tester may not come out clean because of the melted chocolate in the center.) Leave the cupcakes in the pan on a rack to cool for 5 to 10 minutes. Transfer the cupcakes to the wire rack to cool completely before continuing, about 1 hour.

Cupcake Construction: Place the cupcakes back in the pans, and top each cupcake first with an 1½-inch square of milk chocolate and then ½ of a giant marshmallow or ¼ cup mini-sized marshmallows. Place one pan of cupcakes at a time under the broiler for 1 to 2 minutes, watching carefully, until the marshmallows are puffed and lightly browned.

You may have to move the pan around a little to evenly brown the tops. If using the giant marshmallows, cool slightly and press the top of each marshmallow down lightly to cover the top of the cupcake. Cupcakes can be refrigerated for up to 3 days in an airtight container, or frozen for 1 month.

Power tool alert! Use that baby blowtorch to brown the marshmallows to perfection, but be careful!

MIX AND MATCH: Camp Out's Cake with No-Hitter's Best Chocolate Buttercream (page 89)

Camp Out's S'more's Topping with Triple Play's Slammin' Chocolate Cake (page 84)

[NOTES]

_____

_____

_____

_____

_____

_____

_____

....

[BUTCH'S BAKING LESSON] The Oven (Part 2): Ovens are notorious for having hot and cool spots in them, which means that your cupcakes won't bake evenly. And the high-end ones are not exempt. If you have a convection feature, that will lessen the problem, but we don't recommend convection with these cupcakes. So the best way to solve the problem is by rotating the pans, not only side-to-side, but back-to-front as well.

CAMP OUT ::

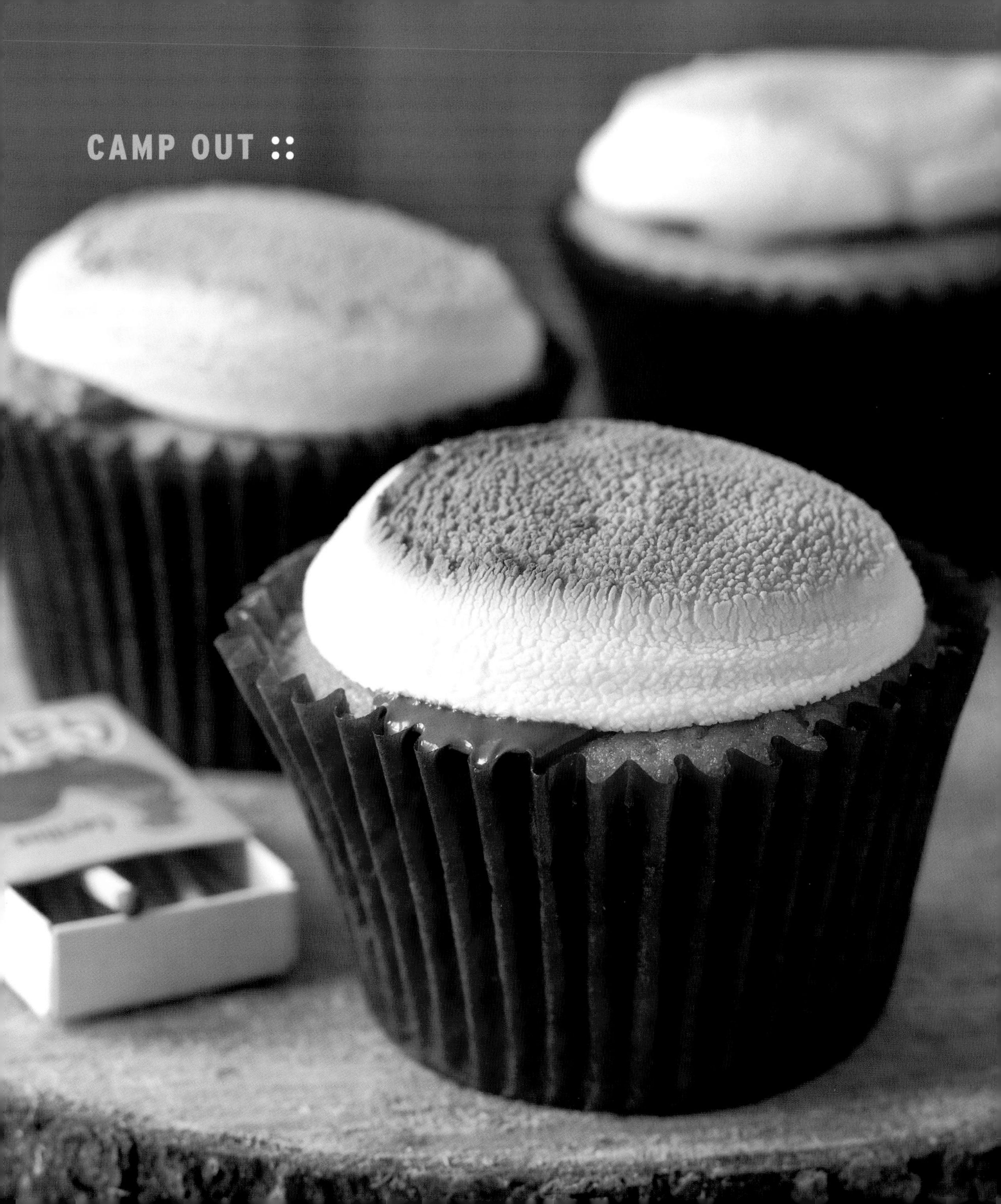

5:
COUPLES' NIGHT OUT

DATE NIGHT ::

DATE NIGHT ::

A Date and Fig Cream Cupcake with Lemon Cream Cheese Frosting Let's face it: Dates are special. You get dressed up a little more. You want to put your best foot forward. This combo of dates and figs is just that. It may require a little more prep work, but it's not your ordinary cupcake. It's something a little more special. Inspired by John's Italian grandma's recipe that she only served on special occasions, they're made with heavy cream and a hint of orange. They're tender and moist and topped with our lemony cream cheese frosting—worthy of any Saturday night. Plus, we've made the cake an easy one-bowl recipe: it's all done in a food processor. [MAKES 12 CUPCAKES]

INGREDIENT ROSTER:

For the Date and Fig Cream Cupcakes:

- ½ cup pitted dates (10 to 12)
- ½ cup dried figs (10 to 12), such as Black Mission, stems removed
- ⅓ cup sugar
- ⅓ cup firmly packed dark brown sugar
- 6 tablespoons (¾ stick) unsalted butter, melted and cooled slightly
- 2 large eggs, broken into a small bowl
- ½ cup heavy cream
- ½ cup full-fat sour cream
- ⅓ cup whole milk
- 2 teaspoons pure vanilla extract
- ¾ teaspoon grated orange zest, from 1 large orange
- 1 cup unbleached all-purpose flour

- ¾ teaspoon baking powder
- ¾ teaspoon baking soda
- ¼ teaspoon salt
- ⅔ cup coarsely chopped walnuts

For Lemon Cream Cheese Frosting:

- 12 tablespoons (1½ sticks) unsalted butter, softened
- 9 ounces cream cheese, softened (three 3-ounce packages)
- 3 cups confectioners' sugar, sifted through a strainer
- 1½ tablespoons heavy cream
- 1½ teaspoons pure vanilla extract
- 1½ teaspoons grated lemon zest, from 1 large lemon

PLAN OF ATTACK:

Make the Cupcakes: Place a baking rack in the center of the oven and preheat the oven to 350°F. Line two 6-cup jumbo-size muffin pans with liners and set aside.

In the bowl of a food processor, combine the dates, figs, sugar, and dark brown sugar, processing until the fruit is finely ground, about 45 seconds. Add the melted butter, eggs, heavy cream, sour cream, milk, vanilla, and orange zest, processing for 20 to 30 seconds more. Scrape down the sides of the bowl. Place a strainer over the workbowl and sift the flour, baking powder, baking soda, and salt directly into it. Add the walnuts. Pulse about 12 times, just until combined.

Fill each prepared muffin cup with ⅓ cup batter, about ⅔ full. Bake, rotating the pans halfway through, until the tops are just firm to the touch and a tester inserted in the center of a cupcake comes out clean, about 25 minutes. Leave the cupcakes in the pan on a rack to cool for 5 to 10 minutes. Transfer the cupcakes to the wire rack to cool completely before frosting, about 1 hour.

Make the Frosting: In a large-size mixing bowl, with an electric mixer on medium-high speed, beat the butter and cream cheese until light and fluffy. Scrape down the sides of the bowl, reduce the speed to medium, and add half of the confectioners' sugar, the heavy cream, vanilla, and lemon zest, beating to incorporate. Add the rest of the confectioners' sugar, beating on medium-high for 2 to 3 minutes until very smooth and creamy, scraping down the sides of the bowl as needed.

Cupcake Construction: Get out that ice cream scoop (2 to 2¼ inches in diameter) and top each cupcake with a generous rounded scoop of frosting. Cupcakes can be refrigerated for up to 3 days in an airtight container, or frozen for 1 month.

If You Like: You can shine them up a bit by taking a butter knife (no serrated edges, please) and pushing the frosting down to about an inch high, flattening the top, and then taking the knife and making a flat 45-degree angled edge all the way around the side of the scoop of frosting.

MIX AND MATCH: Date Night's Cake with Old-Fashioned's Real "Old-Fashioned" Buttercream (page 151)

Date Night's Frosting with Side Car's Lip-Puckering Lemon Cake (page 157)

[NOTES]

_____

_____

_____

_____

_____

_____

_____

_____

_____

_____

_____

_____

[BUTCH'S BAKING LESSON] When grating the rind of citrus fruit, also called zesting, grate only as deep as the color of the fruit. Don't grate the white part underneath, known as the pith, because it has a bitter flavor.

SWEET MAMA ::

Mom's Applejack-Spiked Apple Pie inside a Cinnamon Cupcake topped with Vanilla-Applejack Buttercream When it's fall, it's apple season. Homemade apple pies bring back fond memories for a lot of us at the bakery. Putting homemade apple pie filling inside a cupcake may be a little unconventional, but why not? Making the apples takes a little more effort, but it's worth it because this version of Mom's apple pie won't disappoint. And of course, at Butch's, we just had to spike these cupcakes with some applejack brandy.

[MAKES 12 CUPCAKES]

INGREDIENT ROSTER:

For Mom's Applejack-Spiked Apple Pie Filling:

- ½ cup pure maple syrup
- ¼ cup water
- 2 tablespoons cornstarch
- ¾ teaspoon ground cinnamon
- ⅛ teaspoon salt
- 3 Granny Smith apples, peeled, cored and cut into ¼-inch dice, about 4 cups diced apples
- 1 to 2 tablespoons applejack brandy, such as Laird's

For the Cinnamon Cupcakes:

- 1½ cups unbleached all-purpose flour
- 1½ teaspoons ground cinnamon
- 1 teaspoon baking powder
- ½ teaspoon salt
- 14 tablespoons (1¾ sticks) unsalted butter, softened

- 1 cup plus 2 tablespoons sugar
- 3 large eggs, broken into a small bowl
- 1 teaspoon pure vanilla extract
- ½ cup well-shaken buttermilk
- 2 tablespoons applejack brandy, such as Laird's

For the Vanilla-Applejack Buttercream:

- 10 tablespoons (1¼ sticks) unsalted butter, softened
- 4½ cups confectioners' sugar, sifted through a strainer
- ¼ cup heavy cream
- 1 to 2 tablespoons applejack brandy, such as Laird's
- ½ teaspoon pure vanilla extract
- ⅛ teaspoon salt

PLAN OF ATTACK:

Make the Apple Pie Filling: Preheat the oven to 400°F. In a glass or Pyrex baking dish (a 9-inch pie plate works well), stir together the maple syrup, water, cornstarch, cinnamon, and salt. Add the diced apples and stir to coat. Cover with foil and bake for 30 to 40 minutes until the apples are soft and the liquid is bubbling, stirring once halfway through the cooking time. Cool to room temperature and stir in the applejack. Can be refrigerated for 1 week or frozen for 2 months. Makes 2 cups, enough to fill 24 cupcakes. (An easy substitute is 2 cups of canned apple pie filling, cutting the apples into ¼-inch dice.)

Make the Cupcakes: Place a baking rack in the center of the oven and preheat the oven to 350°F. Line two 6-cup jumbo-size muffin pans with liners and set aside.

Place a strainer over a medium-size mixing bowl and sift together the flour, cinnamon, baking powder, and salt. Set aside.

In another medium-size mixing bowl, with an electric mixer on medium-high speed, beat the butter and sugar together until light and fluffy, 2 to 3 minutes. Scrape down the sides of the bowl, and add the eggs and vanilla, beating until combined. Add about half of the flour mixture, the buttermilk, and applejack brandy, mixing just until all the dry ingredients are incorporated. Add the rest of the flour mixture, and mix just to combine, scraping down the sides of the bowl as needed.

Fill each prepared muffin cup with a rounded ⅓ cup batter, about ¾ full, smoothing the tops. Bake, rotating the pans halfway through, until the tops are just firm to the touch and a tester inserted in the center of a cupcake comes out clean, about 25 minutes. Leave the cupcakes in the pan on a rack to cool for 5 to 10 minutes. Transfer the cupcakes to the wire rack to cool completely before filling and frosting, about 1 hour.

Make the Buttercream: In a large-size mixing bowl, with an electric mixer on medium-high speed, beat the butter until light and fluffy. Scrape down the sides of the bowl, reduce the speed to medium, and add half of the confectioners' sugar, the cream, applejack brandy, vanilla, and salt, beating to incorporate. Add the rest of the confectioners' sugar, beating on medium-high for 2 to 3 minutes until very smooth and creamy, scraping down the sides of the bowl as needed.

Cupcake Construction: With a small knife or melon baller, carve a 2-inch diameter hole in the top of each cupcake. Fill with 1 to 2 tablespoons of the apple filling. Then get out that ice cream scoop (2 to 2¼ inches in diameter) and top each cupcake with frosting. Cupcakes can be refrigerated for up to 3 days in an airtight container, or frozen for 1 month.

If You Like: You can shine them up a bit by taking a butter knife (no serrated edges, please) and pushing the frosting down to about an inch high, flattening the top, and then taking the knife and making a flat 45-degree angled edge all the way around the side of the scoop of frosting.

Virgin Sweet Mama: Omit the applejack in the apple filling. Substitute 2 tablespoons buttermilk for the applejack in the cake, and 1 to 2 tablespoons heavy cream for the applejack in the frosting.

MIX AND MATCH: Sweet Mama's Cake with Big Papi's White Chocolate–Rum Raisin Buttercream (page 127)
  SweetMama's Buttercream with Driller's Maple Cake (page 46)

....

[BUTCH'S BAKING LESSON] Have fun! Baking cupcakes isn't supposed to be stressful or hard work. You're making something delicious to eat, man. Enjoy the journey!

OLD-FASHIONED ::

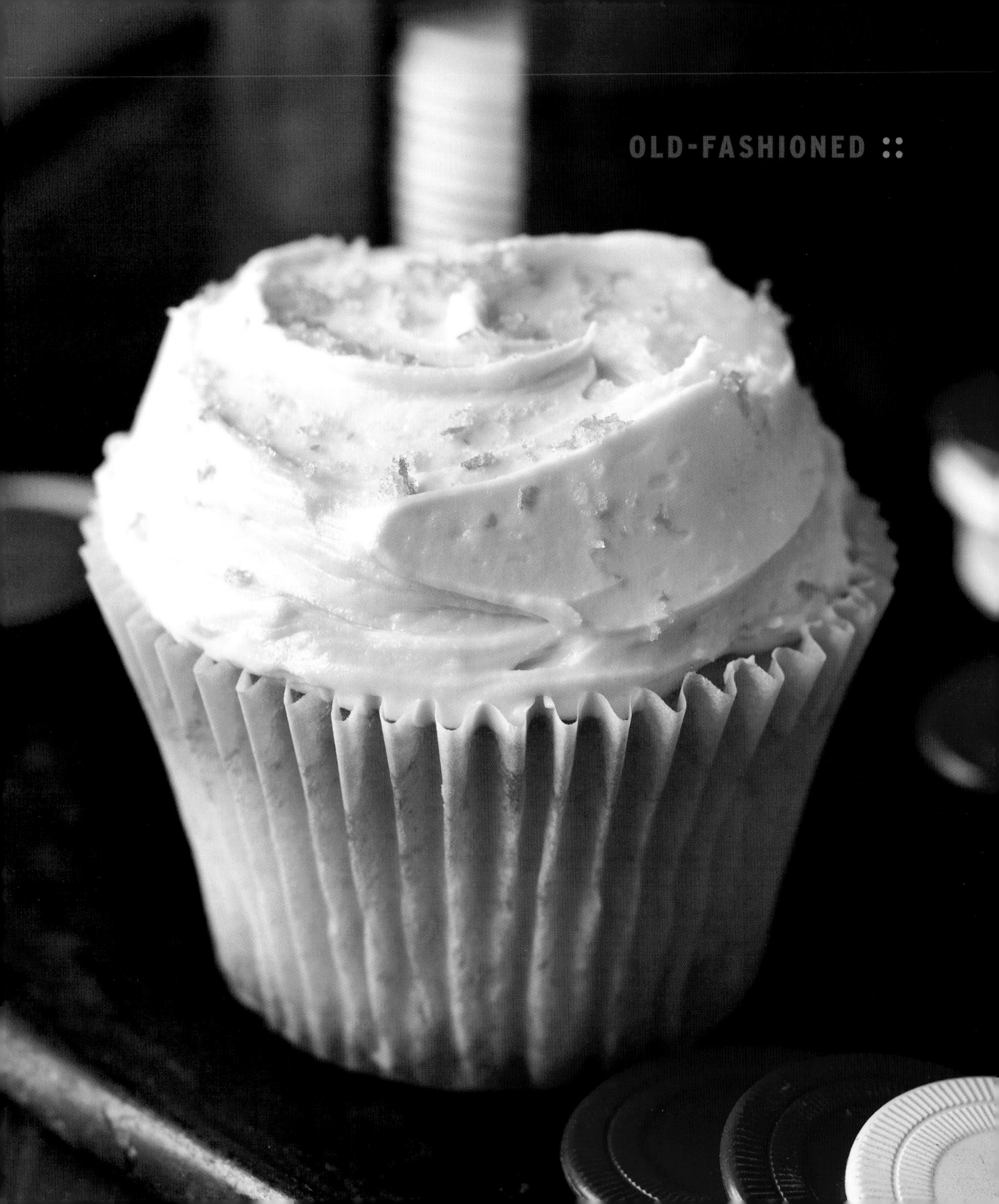

OLD-FASHIONED ::

Whiskey-Soaked Extreme Orange Cupcake with Real "Old-Fashioned" Buttercream We occasionally enjoy a traditional cocktail at Butch's. And even though this cupcake may be called old-fashioned, it certainly isn't in our book. We pack the cupcake with an extreme amount of real orange, soak it in whiskey. Our choice? Jack Daniel's. Then top it with an authentic "Old-Fashioned" buttercream. Just like the cocktail itself, this creamy concoction has whiskey, Angostura bitters, and a hint of orange. All that's missing is that red maraschino cherry on top. We're not too fond of those, but go for it if you must. [MAKES 12 CUPCAKES]

INGREDIENT ROSTER:

For the Extreme Orange Cupcakes:

- 1½ cups plus 2 tablespoons cake flour
- 1½ teaspoons baking powder
- ½ teaspoon salt
- 12 tablespoons (1½ sticks) unsalted butter, softened
- 1¼ cups sugar
- 3 large eggs, broken into a small bowl
- ¼ cup plus 2 tablespoons freshly squeezed orange juice, from 3 large oranges
- 1 tablespoon orange zest, from 1 large orange
- ¼ teaspoon orange extract
- 1 teaspoon pure vanilla extract
- ¼ cup full-fat sour cream

For the Real "Old-Fashioned" Buttercream:

- 12 tablespoons (1½ sticks) unsalted butter, softened
- 4½ cups confectioners' sugar, sifted through a strainer
- ¼ cup plus 2 tablespoons whiskey, such as Jack Daniel's
- 9 dashes Angostura bitters
- ¾ teaspoon orange extract
- ½ teaspoon orange zest

For the Soaking Liquid:

- ¼ to ½ cup whiskey, such as Jack Daniel's

Topping: (optional)

- **Orange Sawdust (recipe follows)**

PLAN OF ATTACK:

Make the Cupcakes: Place a baking rack in the center of the oven and preheat the oven to 350°F. Line two 6-cup jumbo-size muffin pans with liners and set aside.

Place a strainer over a medium-size mixing bowl and sift together the cake flour, baking powder, and salt. Set aside.

In another medium-size mixing bowl, with an electric mixer on medium-high speed, beat the butter and sugar together until light and fluffy, 2 to 3 minutes. Scrape down the sides of the bowl, and add the eggs, beating until combined. Add the flour mixture, orange juice, orange zest, orange extract, and vanilla, beating on low speed just until all the dry ingredients are incorporated. Add the sour cream and beat again to incorporate, scraping down the sides of the bowl as needed.

Fill each prepared muffin cup with a rounded ⅓ cup batter, about ¾ full. Bake, rotating the pans halfway through, until the tops are just firm to the touch and a tester inserted in the center of a cupcake comes out clean, about 24 minutes. Leave the cupcakes in the pan on a rack to cool for 5 to 10 minutes. Transfer the cupcakes to the wire rack to cool completely before frosting, about 1 hour.

Make the Buttercream: In a large-size mixing bowl, with an electric mixer on medium-high speed, beat the butter until light and fluffy. Scrape down the sides of the bowl, reduce the speed to medium, and add half of the confectioners' sugar, the whiskey, bitters, orange extract, and orange zest, beating to incorporate. Add the rest of the confectioners' sugar, beating on medium-high for 2 to 3 minutes until very smooth and creamy, scraping down the sides of the bowl as needed.

Cupcake Construction: Using a wooden skewer, poke about 15 holes in the top of each cupcake and slowly spoon 1 to 2 teaspoons of the whiskey over the top of each cupcake. Let them sit for 10 minutes to allow the whiskey to be absorbed. Now get out that ice cream scoop (2 to 2¼ inches in diameter) and top each cupcake with frosting. Sprinkle the tops with ¼ to ½ teaspoon of the orange sawdust, if desired. Cupcakes can be refrigerated for up to 3 days in an airtight container, or frozen for 1 month.

If You Like: Before sprinkling the tops, you can shine them up a bit by taking a butter knife (no serrated edges, please) and pushing the frosting down to about an inch high, flattening the top, and then taking the knife and making a flat 45-degree angled edge all the way around the side of the scoop of frosting.

Virgin Old-Fashioned: Use the Extreme Orange Cake and substitute ¼ cup heavy cream plus 2 tablespoons fresh-squeezed orange juice for the whiskey and bitters in the frosting.

Orange Sawdust: In a small bowl, mix together 2 tablespoons sugar and ½ teaspoon grated orange zest.

MIX AND MATCH: Old-Fashioned's Cake with Side Car's "Side Car" Buttercream (page 157)
   Old-Fashioned's Buttercream with Kick-Off's Moist Carrot-Pineapple Cake (page 98)

....

[BUTCH'S BAKING LESSON] Used your baking soda and baking powder lately? Well if you haven't, chances are they won't make your cupcakes rise the way they should. To test them, pour a little water on the baking powder or a little vinegar on the baking soda, and see if they bubble up. If they don't, fling them and buy fresh. As a matter of fact, if you're in doubt, they're inexpensive items. Just buy new.

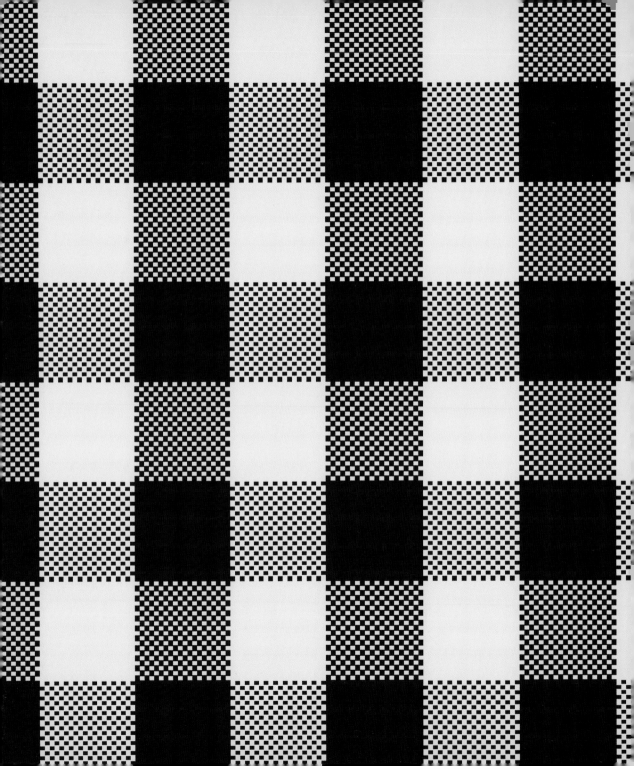

"Have fun! Baking cupcakes isn't supposed to be stressful or hard work. You're making something delicious to eat, man. Enjoy the journey."

SIDE CAR

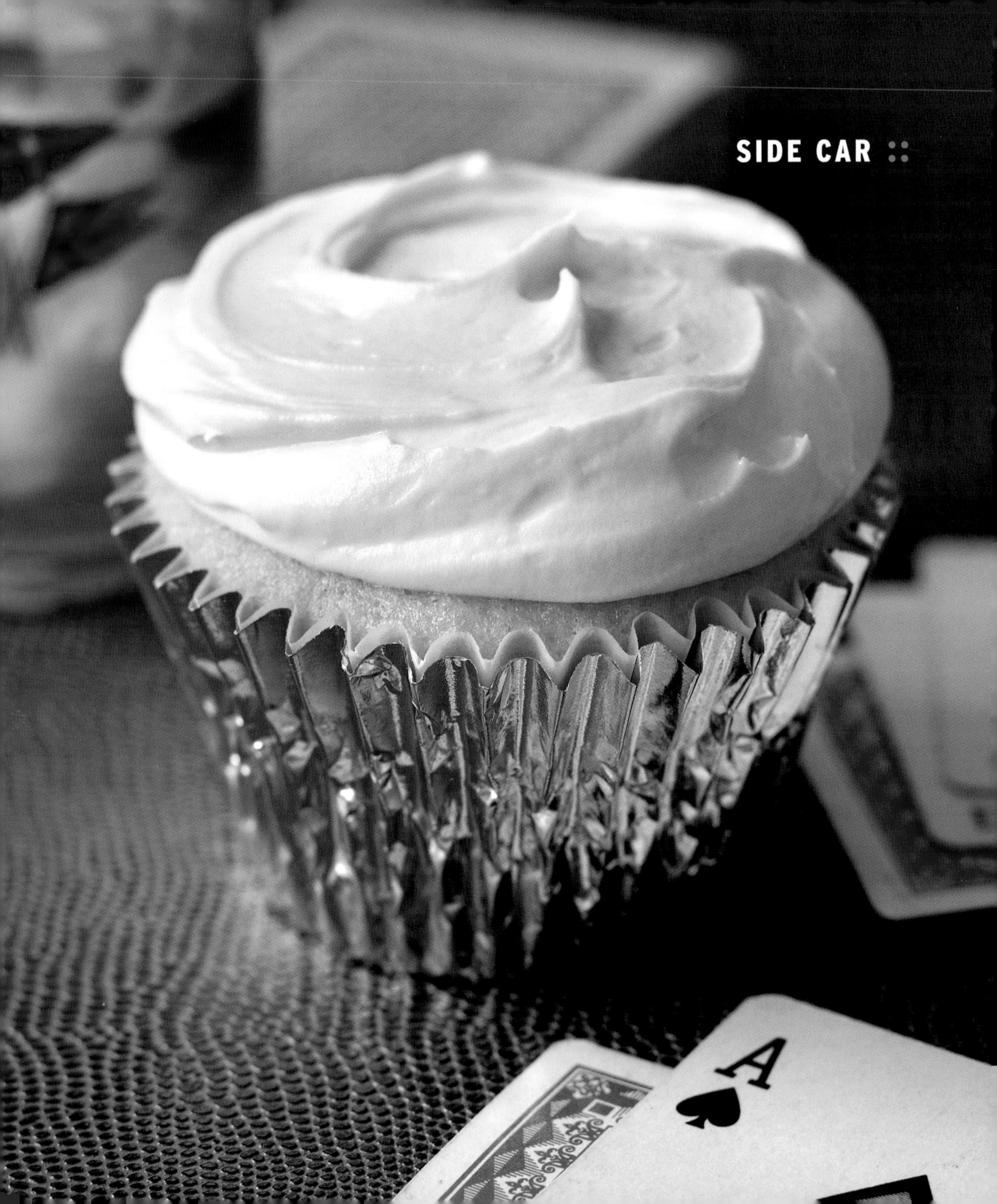

SIDE CAR ::

A Brandy-Soaked Lip-Puckering Lemon Cupcake with "Side Car" Buttercream
The Side Car cocktail is said to have been created at the Ritz Men's Bar in Paris after an air raid during World War I. Can you get more manly than that? In honor of this delicious cocktail, we created an extra-lemony cupcake that we soak in French brandy and top with our "Side Car" buttercream. The original recipe calls for equal parts Cointreau, brandy, and fresh lemon juice, and that's just what you'll find on the top of this cupcake too. [MAKES 12 CUPCAKES]

INGREDIENT ROSTER:

For the Lip-Puckering Lemon Cupcakes:

- 1½ cups unbleached all-purpose flour
- 1½ teaspoons baking powder
- ½ teaspoon salt
- 12 tablespoons (1½ sticks) unsalted butter, softened
- 1¼ cups sugar
- 3 large eggs, broken into a small bowl
- ¼ cup plus 2 tablespoons freshly squeezed lemon juice
- 1 tablespoon grated lemon zest, from 2 to 3 lemons
- 1 teaspoon pure vanilla extract
- ¼ cup plus 2 tablespoons full-fat sour cream

For the "Side Car" Buttercream:

- 12 tablespoons (1½ sticks) unsalted butter, softened
- 4½ cups confectioners' sugar, sifted through a strainer
- 2 tablespoons plus 2 teaspoons brandy
- 2 tablespoons Cointreau or other orange liqueur
- 2 tablespoons fresh lemon juice

For the Soaking Liquid:

- ¼ to ½ cup brandy, such as Raynal French

PLAN OF ATTACK:

Make the Cupcakes: Place a baking rack in the center of the oven and preheat the oven to 350°F. Line two 6-cup jumbo-size muffin pans with liners and set aside.

Place a strainer over a medium-size mixing bowl and sift together the flour, baking powder, and salt. Set aside.

In another medium-size mixing bowl, with an electric mixer on medium-high speed, beat the butter and sugar together until light and fluffy, 2 to 3 minutes. Scrape down the sides of the bowl, and add the eggs, beating until combined. Add the flour mixture, lemon juice, lemon zest, and vanilla, beating on low speed, just until all the dry ingredients are incorporated. Beat in the sour cream last, scraping down the sides of the bowl as needed. The batter will be thick.

Fill each prepared muffin cup with a rounded ⅓ cup batter, about ¾ full, smoothing the tops. Bake, rotating the pans halfway through, until the tops are just firm to the touch and a tester inserted in the center of a cupcake comes out clean, about 24 minutes. Leave the cupcakes in the pan on a rack to cool for 5 to 10 minutes. Transfer the cupcakes to the wire rack to cool completely before continuing, about 1 hour.

Make the Buttercream: In a large-size mixing bowl, using an electric mixer on medium-high speed, beat the butter until light and fluffy. Add half of the confectioners' sugar, the brandy, Cointreau, and lemon juice, beating until smooth. Add the rest of the confectioners' sugar and continue to beat on medium-high speed until thick and creamy, 2 to 3 minutes, scraping down the sides of the bowl as needed.

Cupcake Construction: Using a wooden skewer, poke about 15 holes in the top of each cupcake and slowly spoon 1 to 2 teaspoons of the brandy over the top of each cupcake. Let them sit for 10 minutes to allow the brandy to be absorbed. Now get out that ice cream scoop (2 to 2¼ inches in diameter) and top each cupcake with frosting. Cupcakes can be refrigerated for up to 3 days in an airtight container, or frozen for 1 month.

If You Like: You can shine them up a bit by taking a butter knife (no serrated edges, please) and pushing the frosting down to about an inch high, flattening the top, and then taking the knife and making a flat 45-degree angled edge all the way around the side of the scoop of frosting.

Virgin Side Car: Make the Lip-Puckering Lemon cupcakes, then make the frosting, substituting ¼ cup heavy cream for the brandy and Cointreau.

MIX AND MATCH: Side Car's Cake with Triple Play's Really Rich Chocolate Ganache (page 84)

Side Car's Buttercream with Coco Loco's Coconut-Swirled Coconut Cake (page 160)

[NOTES]

_____

_____

_____

_____

_____

_____

_____

_____

....

[BUTCH'S BAKING LESSON] Nothing imitation!: At Butch's we don't use anything other than the real thing; nothing imitation here. So you're going to have to squeeze those lemons and limes, grate those zests, and use only the purest of extracts to get the best flavor out of your cupcakes. Promise us you'll do that.

COCO LOCO ::

A Coconut-Swirled Coconut Cupcake topped with Coconut-Cream Cheese Frosting and Even More Coconut At Butch's we're all about bold flavors. We tried all different ways to give these cupcakes a bigger coconut punch without much luck. And then one day Janice said, "Why not add a layer of the coconut right through the center of the cupcake while it bakes?" What a great idea! We top them with our cream cheese frosting that we've switched up with more coconut flavor, and top that with lots more sweet flaky coconut to boot. A hit in anyone's book! [MAKES 12 CUPCAKES]

INGREDIENT ROSTER:

For the Coconut-Swirled Coconut Cupcakes:

- 1¼ cups plus 2 tablespoons unbleached all-purpose flour
- ½ teaspoon baking powder
- ½ teaspoon baking soda
- ⅛ teaspoon salt
- 8 tablespoons (1 stick) unsalted butter, softened
- ¾ cup sugar
- 2 large eggs, broken into a small bowl
- 1½ teaspoons pure vanilla extract
- ½ cup well-shaken buttermilk
- ½ cup cream of coconut, such as Coco Lopez, melted
- ¾ to 1 cup sweetened flaked coconut

For the Coconut Cream Cheese Frosting:

- 12 tablespoons (1½ sticks) unsalted butter, softened
- 6 ounces cream cheese, softened
- 3 cups confectioners' sugar, sifted through a strainer
- 3 tablespoons cream of coconut, such as Coco Lopez
- 1½ teaspoons pure vanilla extract
- ¼ teaspoon salt

Topping:

- 1½ to 2 cups sweetened flaked coconut

PLAN OF ATTACK:

Make the Cupcakes: Place a baking rack in the center of the oven and preheat the oven to 350°F. Line two 6-cup jumbo-size muffin pans with liners and set aside.

Place a strainer over a medium-size mixing bowl and sift together the flour, baking powder, baking soda, and salt. Set aside.

In another medium-size mixing bowl, with an electric mixer on medium-high speed, beat the butter and sugar together until light and fluffy, 2 to 3 minutes. Scrape down the sides of the bowl, and add the eggs and vanilla, beating until combined. Add the flour mixture and the buttermilk, and beat on low speed, just until all the dry ingredients are incorporated. Add the cream of coconut and mix just until well combined, scraping down the sides of the bowl as needed.

Fill each prepared muffin cup by layering 2 tablespoons of batter, then 1 tablespoon of flaked coconut, and finally another 2 tablespoons of batter into each cup. Bake, rotating the pans halfway through, until the tops are just firm to the touch and a tester inserted in the center of a cupcake comes out clean, about 23 minutes. Leave the cupcakes in the pan on a rack to cool for 5 to 10 minutes. Transfer the cupcakes to the wire rack to cool completely before frosting, about 1 hour.

Make the Frosting: In a large-size mixing bowl, with an electric mixer on medium-high speed, beat the butter and cream cheese until light and fluffy. Scrape down the sides of the bowl, reduce the speed to medium, and add half of the confectioners' sugar, the cream of coconut, vanilla, and salt, beating to incorporate. Add the rest of the confectioners' sugar, beating on medium-high for 2 to 3 minutes until very smooth and creamy, scraping down the sides of the bowl as needed.

Cupcake Construction:

Get out that ice cream scoop (2 to 2¼ inches in diameter) and top each cupcake with a generous rounded scoop of frosting. Top each cupcake with a heaping tablespoon of the coconut. Cupcakes can be refrigerated for up to 3 days in an airtight container, or frozen for 1 month.

If You Like: Before sprinkling with the coconut, you can shine the cupcakes up a bit by taking a butter knife (no serrated edges, please) and pushing the frosting down to about an inch high, flattening the top, and then taking the knife and making a flat 45-degree angled edge all the way around the side of the scoop of frosting.

MIX AND MATCH: Coco Loco's Cake with Date Night's Lemon Cream Cheese Frosting (page 143)
Coco Loco's Frosting with Kick-Off's Moist Carrot-Pineapple Cake (page 98)

[NOTES]

_____

_____

_____

_____

_____

_____

_____

_____

....

[BUTCH'S BAKING LESSON] When you buy cream of coconut, you will find that when you open the can, it will most likely be solid. In order to use it in a recipe, it needs to be a liquid. So, if it is solid, scoop out approximately what you will need into a small saucepan, and stir it over low heat until melted. Anything left over can be refrigerated for up 2 weeks.

COCO LOCO ::

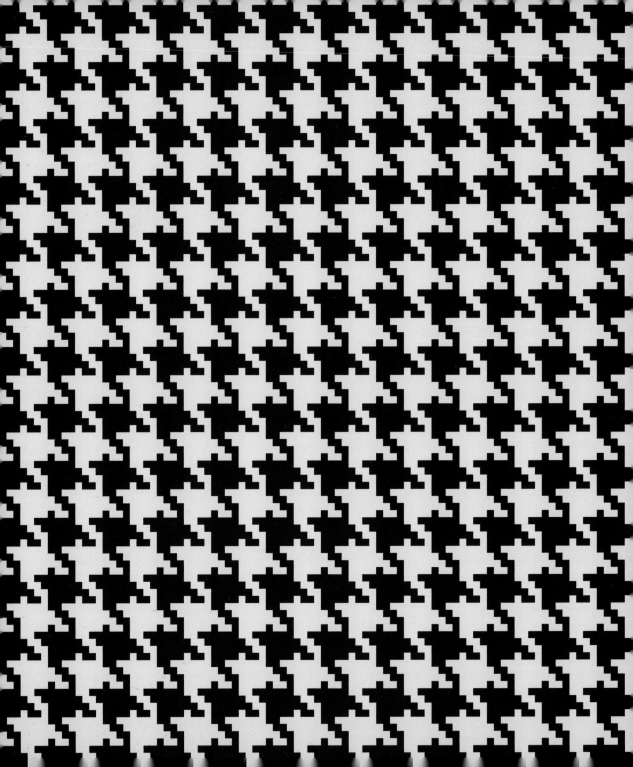

6.

BUTCH'S ON-THE-GO
USING PRE-MADE CAKE MIXES

RUM RUNNER ::

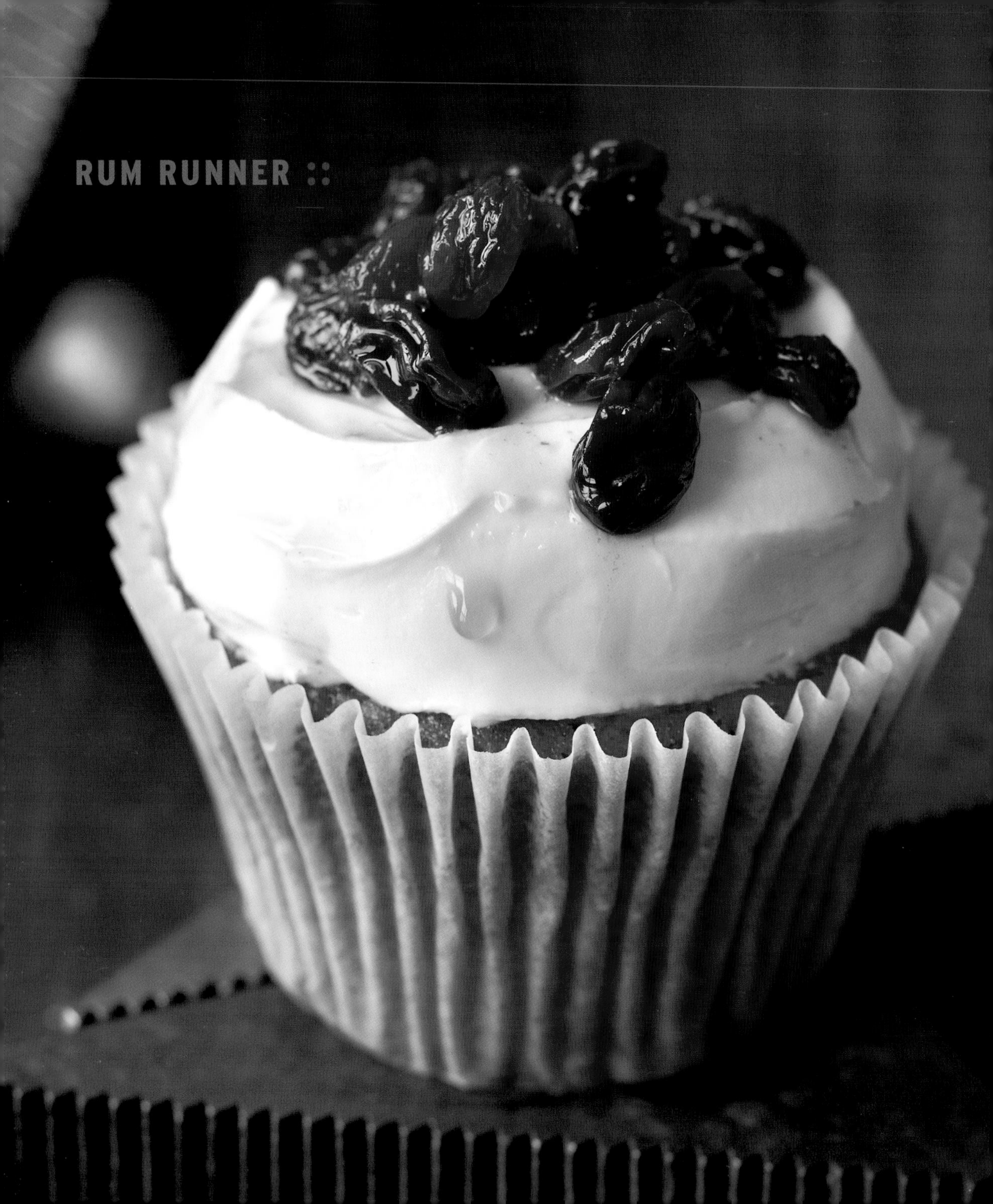

RUM RUNNER ::

A Rum-Raisin Cupcake topped with Rum Cream Cheese Frosting

This one couldn't be easier. Lots of rum in the mix, a can of vanilla frosting, and some cream cheese, and you're on your way. We suggest making a lot of the rum raisins in advance (they'll last for weeks in the fridge), so when you're craving these cupcakes, you'll be ready to go. But don't let that stop you. You can always substitute regular raisins for the rum-soaked version if you're really in a hurry. **[MAKES 18 CUPCAKES]**

INGREDIENT ROSTER:

For the Rum Raisins:

- 1   cup seedless raisins
- ⅔   cup dark rum, such as Mount Gay

For the Rum-Raisin Cupcakes:

- 1   18.25-ounce package spice cake mix, such as Betty Crocker
- 1   3.4-ounce package instant vanilla pudding mix, such as Jell-O
- 3   large eggs, broken into a small bowl
- ¾   cup water
- ½   cup vegetable oil
- ¼   cup dark rum, reserved from rum raisins

For the Rum Cream Cheese Frosting:

- 1   16-ounce can store-bought vanilla frosting, such as Pillsbury Creamy Supreme Vanilla
- 2   8-ounce packages cream cheese, softened
- 8   tablespoons (1 stick) unsalted butter, softened
- 2   tablespoons dark rum, reserved from rum raisins
- 1   teaspoon pure vanilla extract

PLAN OF ATTACK:

Make the Rum Raisins: In a small bowl, combine the raisins and rum and let sit for 15 to 30 minutes. The longer they soak, the more rum flavor they will have. To use, drain very well, squeezing out the rum. Reserve ¼ cup plus 2 tablespoons of the leftover rum for the cake batter and frosting.

Make the Cupcakes: Place a baking rack in the center of the oven and preheat the oven to 350°F. Line three 6-cup jumbo-size muffin pans with liners and set aside.

In a large-size mixing bowl, add all of the cupcake ingredients. With an electric mixer on low speed, mix for 30 seconds to combine, and then beat on medium-high for 2 to 3 minutes more, scraping down the sides of the bowl as needed. Stir in the rum raisins.

Fill each of the prepared muffin cups with no more than ¼ cup batter, about ½ full. Bake, rotating the pans halfway through, until the tops are just firm to the touch and a tester inserted in the center of a cupcake comes out clean, about 22 minutes. Leave the cupcakes in the pan on a rack to cool for 5 to 10 minutes. Transfer the cupcakes to the wire rack to cool completely before frosting, about 1 hour.

Make the Frosting: In a large-size mixing bowl, with an electric mixer on medium-high speed, beat all of the frosting ingredients together for 2 to 3 minutes until very smooth and creamy, scraping down the sides of the bowl as needed.

Cupcake Construction: Get out that ice cream scoop (2 to 2¼ inches in diameter) and top each cupcake with a generous rounded scoop of frosting. Cupcakes can be refrigerated for up to 3 days in an airtight container, or frozen for 1 month.

If You Like: You can shine them up a bit by taking a butter knife (no serrated edges, please) and pushing the frosting down to about an inch high, flattening the top, and then taking the knife and making a flat 45-degree angled edge all the way around the side of the scoop of frosting.

Topping Idea:

Double the rum raisin recipe and scoop 1 tablespoon of the raisins on the top of each cupcake.

[NOTES]

....

[BUTCH'S BAKING LESSON] Freezing unfrosted cupcakes is the best way to keep them fresh. Even if it's overnight, pack them in airtight containers until you need them, defrosting at room temperature.

ICE CREAM CAKE ::

A Chocolate "Ice Cream" Cupcake filled with your Favorite Ice Cream and topped with Chocolate Sauce The name for these cupcakes is a little deceiving, because not only is there ice cream on top of the cupcakes, but there's also melted ice cream in the batter, too! You can choose any flavor cake mix and ice cream combo you want, as well as any toppings that suit your fancy. The ice cream in the batter gives these cupcakes a soft, pillowy texture that really goes well with the frozen ice cream. We like to slice off the top of each cupcake, and place a big scoop of ice cream with a drizzle of chocolate sauce between the 2 pieces of cake. Make these for your next barbecue and watch them go. You'll probably have to whip up a second batch, which will be easy to do, because it's a mix! **[MAKES 18 CUPCAKES]**

INGREDIENT ROSTER:

For the Chocolate "Ice Cream" Cupcakes:

- 1 18.25-ounce package chocolate cake mix, such as Betty Crocker Devil's Food
- 3 large eggs, broken into a small bowl
- 1 cup melted ice cream (we like to use chocolate), about 1¼ cups frozen
- 4 tablespoons (½ stick) unsalted butter, melted and cooled slightly
- 2 teaspoons pure vanilla extract

Toppings:

- 2 quarts of your favorite ice cream
- 1 jar store-bought chocolate sauce, or any sauce you like

PLAN OF ATTACK:

Make the Cupcakes: Place a baking rack in the center of the oven and preheat the oven to 350°F. Line three 6-cup jumbo-size muffin pans with liners and set aside.

In a large-size mixing bowl, add all of the cupcake ingredients. With an electric mixer on low speed, mix for 30 seconds to combine, and then beat on medium-high for 2 to 3 minutes more, scraping down the sides of the bowl as needed. The batter will be very thick.

Fill each prepared muffin cup with no more than ¼ cup batter, about ½ full. Bake, rotating the pans halfway through, until the tops are just firm to the touch and a tester inserted in the center of a cupcake comes out clean, about 24 minutes. Leave the cupcakes in the pan on a rack to cool for 5 to 10 minutes. Transfer the cupcakes to the wire rack to cool completely before frosting, about 1 hour.

Cupcake Construction: Peel back the liner and slice off the top of each cupcake, about half of the way down, and place a scoop of your favorite ice cream along with a drizzle of chocolate sauce in between the pieces of cake. Drizzle the tops with more chocolate sauce. Serve immediately. Unfilled cupcakes can be refrigerated for up to 3 days in an airtight container, or frozen for 1 month.

[NOTES]

_____

_____

_____

_____

_____

_____

_____

_____

_____

_____

_____

_____

_____

_____

_____

_____

_____

_____

[BUTCH'S BAKING LESSON] Don't forget to scrape the sides of the bowl down occasionally. You want to make sure that all of the ingredients are mixed together. In the recipes we remind you over and over, so you don't forget.

ICE CREAM CAKE ::

JACK DANIEL'S RUSH

JACK DANIEL'S RUSH ::

A Red Velvet Cupcake with Jack Daniel's Cream Cheese Frosting Jack Daniel's and Red Velvet just seem to go together at Butch's. We didn't even know that a premade mix existed for red velvet cake, but it does. And after we were finished adding our spin on the mix, you've got to believe it was delicious. If you don't have time for our homemade version, this will do the trick. Topped with a Jack Daniel's and cream cheese frosting, these cupcakes will make everybody happy—everyone over the age of 18, of course.

[MAKES 18 CUPCAKES]

INGREDIENT ROSTER:

For the Red Velvet Cupcakes:

- 1 18.25-ounce package red velvet cake mix, such as Duncan Hines
- 3 large eggs, broken into a small bowl
- 1 cup half-and-half
- 4 tablespoons (½ stick) unsalted butter, melted and cooled slightly
- 2 tablespoons Jack Daniel's whiskey
- 2 teaspoons pure vanilla extract

For the Jack Daniel's Cream Cheese Frosting:

- 1 16-ounce can store-bought vanilla frosting, such as Pillsbury Creamy Supreme Vanilla
- 2 8-ounce packages cream cheese, softened
- 8 tablespoons (1 stick) unsalted butter, softened
- ¼ cup Jack Daniel's whiskey

PLAN OF ATTACK:

Make the Cupcakes: Place a baking rack in the center of the oven and preheat the oven to 350°F. Line three 6-cup jumbo-size muffin pans with liners and set aside.

In a large-size mixing bowl, add all of the cupcake ingredients. With an electric mixer on low speed, mix for 30 seconds to combine, and then beat on medium-high for 2 to 3 minutes more, scraping down the sides of the bowl as needed.

Fill each prepared muffin cup with no more than ¼ cup batter, about ½ full. Bake, rotating the pans halfway through, until the tops are just firm to the touch and a tester inserted in the center of a cupcake comes out clean, about 23 minutes. Leave the cupcakes in the pan on a rack to cool for 5 to 10 minutes. Transfer the cupcakes to the wire rack to cool completely before frosting, about 1 hour.

Make the Frosting: In a medium-size mixing bowl, with an electric mixer on medium-high speed, beat all of the frosting ingredients together for 2 to 3 minutes until very smooth and creamy, scraping down the sides of the bowl as needed.

Cupcake Construction: Get out that ice cream scoop (2 to 2¼ inches in diameter) and top each cupcake with a generous rounded scoop of frosting. Cupcakes can be refrigerated for up to 3 days in an airtight container, or frozen for 1 month.

If You Like: You can shine them up a bit by taking a butter knife (no serrated edges, please) and pushing the frosting down to about an inch high, flattening the top, and then taking the knife and making a flat 45-degree angled edge all the way around the side of the scoop of frosting.

[NOTES]

_____

_____

_____

_____

_____

_____

_____

_____

_____

_____

_____

_____

_____

_____

_____

_____

[BUTCH'S BAKING LESSON] Don't ever use salted butter in baking. Different brands of butter may have different amounts of salt in their salted butter. By using unsalted butter, you can control the amount of salt in your recipe. Plus, salt is a preservative, so salted butter can sit on your grocer's shelf longer without going rancid. That means that unsalted butter will most times be fresher.

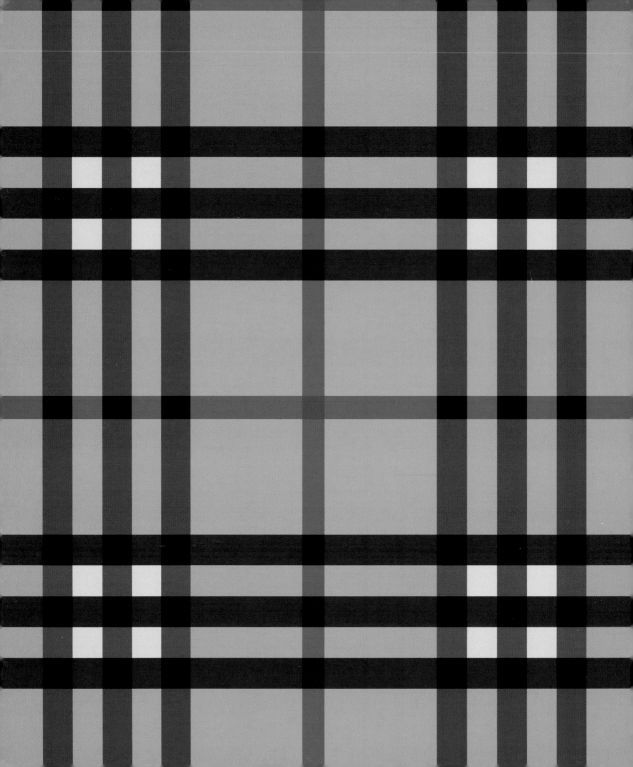

"Play with your food. The sky's the limit. Be creative. Get Butch with your cupcakes!"

NEW YAWK CREAM PIE ::

NEW YAWK CREAM PIE ::

A Yellow Butter Cupcake filled with Vanilla Pudding and topped with an Easy Chocolate Glaze We know that sometimes you want a cupcake, but time is of the essence. So here's an easy way to cut out the middleman and get right to the nitty-gritty. Choose the butter version of a boxed yellow cake mix for these cupcakes. We've switched up the ingredients here so that you won't even know these cupcakes came from a mix. Filled with store-bought vanilla pudding and topped with our super-easy chocolate glaze, you'll impress all of your friends, and no one will be the wiser. **[MAKES 18 CUPCAKES]**

INGREDIENT ROSTER:

For the Yellow Butter Cupcakes:

1 18.25-ounce package yellow butter cake mix, such as Duncan Hines

3 large eggs, broken into a small bowl

1 cup half-and-half

4 tablespoons (½ stick) unsalted butter, melted and cooled slightly

2 teaspoons pure vanilla extract

For the Vanilla Filling:

4 4-ounce containers store-bought vanilla pudding, such as Swiss Miss

For the Easy Chocolate Glaze:

1 16-ounce can store-bought chocolate fudge frosting, such as Duncan Hines

PLAN OF ATTACK:

Make the Cupcakes: Place a baking rack in the center of the oven and preheat the oven to 350°F. Line three 6-cup jumbo-size muffin pans with liners and set aside.

In a large-size mixing bowl, add all of the cupcake ingredients. With an electric mixer on low speed, mix for 30 seconds to combine, and then beat on medium-high for 2 to 3 minutes more, scraping down the sides of the bowl as needed.

Fill each of the prepared muffin cups with no more than $\frac{1}{4}$ cup batter, about $\frac{1}{2}$ full. Bake, rotating the pans halfway through, until the tops are just firm to the touch and a tester inserted in the center of a cupcake comes out clean, about 22 minutes. Leave the cupcakes in the pan on a rack to cool for 5 to 10 minutes. Transfer the cupcakes to the wire rack to cool completely before filling and frosting, about 1 hour.

Make the Glaze: In a small saucepan, heat the frosting until melted enough to run off a spoon. Let cool slightly to thicken.

Cupcake Construction: Using a small paring knife or melon baller, cut a 2-inch-diameter hole in the top of each cupcake. Reserve the cutout pieces. Fill with pudding almost to the top of the hole, about 1 rounded tablespoon each, and then slice a piece from the reserved cutouts to cover the pudding. Using a measuring tablespoon, spread 1 heaping tablespoon of chocolate glaze over the top of each cupcake. Don't worry if it drips over the sides. Cupcakes can be refrigerated for up to 3 days in an airtight container, or frozen for 1 month.

[NOTES]

_____

_____

_____

_____

_____

_____

_____

_____

_____

_____

_____

_____

_____

_____

_____

_____

_____

_____

_____

_____

[BUTCH'S BAKING LESSON] A teaspoon is not a tablespoon. Don't try to use a spoon out of your utensil drawer to measure. These measuring spoons are very exact. Here's the math: 3 teaspoons equal 1 tablespoon.

PEPPERMINT PATTY ::

A Devil's Food Cupcake stuffed with a Peppermint Patty and frosted with Chocolate-Mint Frosting We're candy freaks at Butch's. One of the ways we satisfy that urge is by putting candy inside our cupcakes. Bite into one of these easy-to-make cupcakes and you'll be shocked how good a piece of candy can taste when it's surrounded by some delicious devil's food and chocolate-mint frosting. **[MAKES 18 CUPCAKES]**

INGREDIENT ROSTER:

For the Devil's Food Cupcakes:

- 1 18.25-ounce package devil's food cake mix, such as Duncan Hines
- 3 large eggs, broken into a small bowl
- 1 cup water
- 1 cup full-fat sour cream
- ⅓ cup mild vegetable oil
- 2 teaspoons pure vanilla extract
- 18 small Peppermint Patties

For the Chocolate-Mint Frosting:

- 1 16-ounce can store-bought chocolate fudge frosting, such as Duncan Hines
- ¾ teaspoon peppermint extract

PLAN OF ATTACK:

Make the Cupcakes: Place a baking rack in the center of the oven and preheat the oven to 350°F. Line three 6-cup jumbo-size muffin pans with liners and set aside.

In a large-size mixing bowl, add all of the cupcake ingredients except the peppermint patties. With an electric mixer on low speed, beat for 30 seconds to combine. Raise the speed to medium-high and beat for 2 to 3 minutes more, scraping down the sides of the bowl as needed.

Fill each prepared muffin cup with 2 rounded tablespoons of batter, center a peppermint patty on top of the batter in each cup, and cover with one more rounded tablespoon of batter, about ¾ full. Bake, rotating the pans halfway through, until the tops are just firm to the touch, about 25 minutes. Leave the cupcakes in the pan on a rack to cool for 5 to 10 minutes. Transfer the cupcakes to the wire rack to cool completely before frosting, about 1 hour.

Make the Frosting: In a small mixing bowl, stir together the frosting and peppermint extract, combining well.

Cupcake Construction: Using a butter knife, spread one heaping tablespoon of frosting on top of each cupcake. Cupcakes can be refrigerated for up to 3 days in an airtight container, or frozen for 1 month.

[NOTES]

_____

_____

_____

_____

_____

_____

_____

_____

_____

_____

_____

_____

_____

_____

_____

_____

_____

[BUTCH'S BAKING LESSON] Now you can follow a recipe. So how about starting to think outside of the box a little? Why not put your own spin on all of these cupcakes? Try substituting different flavor combinations. Sprinkle them with different toppings or stir nuts, fruit, or candy into frostings and make an instant filling. Play with your food. The sky's the limit. Be creative. Get Butch with your cupcakes!

PEPPERMINT PATTY ::

index